Marriage CAN Win!

By

Eric & Dr. Sakeisha Hylick

TDR Brands Publishing
Atlanta

Printed in the United States of America by
TDR Brands Publishing
2221 Peachtree St. NE D249
Atlanta, GA 30309
First Edition: May 2016
Library of Congress Cataloging-in-Publication data is
available upon request.
Book Review and Edit by TDR Brands Publishing
Cover Design by Eralphia Eckles, III

ISBN 978-0-9907516-3-2

Preface

Marriage Can Win is a book based on our experience and desire to support couples who have forgone hardships, heartbreak, and turmoil in their marriage. These marriages would appear to be broken beyond repair with divorce as the final step to end it all. In other words, the marriage was DOOMED, it was over, and somebody refused to reconcile!

It is our heartfelt desire to share with you the triumphs and muddy waters that plagued us into reaching our lowest point in marriage. It is by faith that our experiences and guidance will prepare you with many strategies designed to help you overcome the many challenges faced in your marriage. In this book, we will discuss what causes "The Great Divide" in marriage, with topics pertaining to Communication, Finances, and Sex.

Over the course of being married for 17+ years, isolation, frustration, confusion and rejection were just a few of the emotions experienced which caused us to drift apart. As time progressed, we started to question our decision to get married. In the public eye, we were the happiest most liked couple. We appeared to have it all together on the outside but on the inside we often questioned why we got married to one another.

The challenges before us were job instability, financial challenges, health challenges, and infidelity. I remember saying during one of our conversations, "Lord how much more can we take? "It was at that point; some of the scriptures that we often read together began to, echo repeatedly in our minds, reminding us of the plans that God had for us. Profoundly, we reflected on the same scripture;

Jeremiah 29:11, *"For I know the thoughts and plans that I have for you, says the Lord, thoughts and plans for welfare and peace and not for evil, to give you hope in your final outcome."*

Over 22 years ago at Florida A & M University, in the parking lot of Gaither Gymnasium, we encountered one another and instantly connected, but never knew that it would lead to marriage. We would've never thought that our challenges in marriage would eventually become a guide to supporting other couples in repairing their marriages. We realized that we weren't the only couple hurting, ready to throw in the towel, and quit. Together we decided to be transparent in our challenges in order to help other marriages succeed in areas in which many typically fail. While we could not undo the mistakes that our parents had made, our determination was to stop the revolving cycle by equipping other couples with the necessary tools to work out the kinks in their marriage. One of the key components of succeeded in marriage is being able to walk in forgiveness.

Forgiveness is an essential component in any marriage, it is a process that does not occur instantaneously but it isn't insoluble if you're determined to reconcile. It is our prayer that this book educates, empowers, and encourages couples to walk forward in faith and to win in their marriage.

Acknowledgements

We are thankful to God for our precious children Erica and Xavier, our lives were forever changed when you two were born, and your presence motivates us to strive to be the best mom and dad to you. It is our desire to provide a solid foundation in raising you to continue to be respectful as you grow older. We are so proud of you and thank you for your patience, understanding and support as we grew through this process. You all were a driving force for us during some of the most challenging times in our lives and we are ever so grateful. We love you!

To our mothers, **Dr. Mosezelle White and Altamese Hylick** we want to thank you for your continuous love and support over the years. You truly sacrificed a vast portion of your life to assist us with the children and in whatever manner was necessary to help us succeed. We thank God for you! Your presence in our lives has truly made a tremendous difference and we are eternally grateful.

We also want to thank our Dad **Jack Hylick Jr.** for all your love and support. Love you Papa Smurf! We also want to recognize our Big Sister Brenda Carter, your wisdom, patience and prayers are immeasurable.

There have been so many individuals that have poured into us both individually and as a couple; Deborah & Jude Bien Aime, Deborah & Barrington Hill, Harry Jones, Minister Torres Reed, Coleen Otero and Nakisha Thomas. Last but definitely not least, our business coach, Tierra

Destiny Reid and staff, who encouraged us to continue to press forward until the birth of this book.

We wouldn't be complete without acknowledging Delmar Johnson who helped keep us on task every step of the way.

Author's Bio

Like many married couples today, Eric and Dr. Sakeisha know what it's like to experience challenges in their marriage. After being together for over 22 years and being married for 17 years, they have successfully overcome the challenge of, "The Great Divide in Marriage: Communications, Finance and Sex."

Being offspring of divorced parents, statistically their marriage should not have survived. However, their commitment to winning in marriage has far exceeded any statistical data. Their commitment to the covenant of marriage continuously fuels their desire to help other couples succeed where many typically fail. It is this passion that drives them to continue to help as many marriages as possible in overcoming the odds that lead to divorce.

Dr. Sakeisha was born In Brooklyn, New York and raised in Orangeburg, South Carolina. She has a Doctorate in Pharmacy. Her passion is helping people; particularly couples. Eric, a native Floridian, has an MBA with a concentration in Project Management. He is a proud father, and an exceptional husband. They've been together for 22 years and married for 17+ years. Together they have two very active and loving children; ages 12 and 13.

Eric & Dr. Sakeisha, are very transparent in their conversations regarding how they've overcome obstacles such as bankruptcy, infidelity, unemployment, and communication challenges in their marriage. Their focus was how their experiences could benefit other marriages. According to research, most marriages failed because the only support available was primarily for couples whose marriages were already on life support. The couple immediately took action by finding solutions that provide marriage enrichment guidance.

Eric & Dr. Sakeisha, have been working diligently since 2005 to help marriages move forward in reconciliation. They have served together and individually in ministry for the past 10 years. They've hosted conferences and served as guest speakers at conferences from the East Coast to Hawaii. They've co-founded, Covenant Kingdom Builders, an online teaching ministry. They've also served as facilitators in the Bible Institute and healing ministry at their local home church.

Together Eric and Dr. Sakeisha, have a mission to help *Educate, Empower and Encourage* couples to beat the odds and help their marriage to WIN!

"Every marriage over time goes through challenges and difficulties... But like a precious stone requires polishing to bring out its beauty - it's the loving work of the couple together through those moments that makes it valuable."

— author unknown

Foreward

When you meet people for the first time, we share our surface information - our name, maybe our occupation, whether or not you have kids, and if you are married or not. When you meet people during the transitions of life, it is hard to know what to share with them when you are "becoming". Even surface things may not be as clear as they once were. When I met the Hylick's, I was "becoming". But something about them led me to share more than surface information about myself.

We met at a photoshoot given by our mutual mentor, Tierra Destiny, of TDR Brands International. This photoshoot was unlike any other I have ever been a part of. This photoshoot was not just about the images, the right outfit, or even the celebrity makeovers that we received. This photoshoot was about each of the participants "becoming". We all were involved in one of TDR Brands International Coaching programs and were at the end. This photoshoot was our beginning of what each of us had been working on.

On my drive down to the photoshoot from Columbia, SC to Atlanta, GA, I was speaking to God about so many things, but in particular, I was discussing my marriage. My husband and I were separated for so many reasons, but in particular at that time, we were separated due to domestic violence. Immediately, when things got bad, God told me to stand for my marriage. Though my heart wanted to so badly, my head said no. I struggled with standing for such a broken marriage, but God knew my heart is to serve Him and He knew that I loved my husband. Deep down inside I knew that what my husband and I had become, was not who we were. I could hear God so clearly say to me, "Stand daughter. Not just with your mouth this time, but with your actions." I cried almost the entire 3 and a half hours because my emotions were so high. I was debating with God because so many other things were going right in my life, but my marriage was my sore spot. In that moment on my drive down to celebrate my "becoming" I stopped being lukewarm and decided I was going to continue to move forward. Move forward in my business, move forward with pursing my Masters degree, and move forward and continue to stand for my marriage no matter what it looked like or what I looked like to others for standing.

When I arrived to the photoshoot, no one knew this inner battle that had just happened. They didn't know how God had just lifted so much weight off of me during that drive. There's something about making a decision that will release the weight of not knowing off of you. So I walked into the door not knowing what was waiting for me.

This day was filled with so much empowerment from other women sharing their stories of overcoming while we were being pampered and served like royalty. We were all "becoming" and I think that we all "became" at that Power Photoshoot. It was like we all had made a decision that day to continue to move forward. So in between taking photos, talking, and laughing, I met the Hylick's. We instantly connected. I never have a problem meeting people anyway, but meeting the Hylick's, it was like we were old friends. When we talked they created such a safe space that I opened up about the decision I had just made driving down to Atlanta, GA. I told them that I was standing for my marriage not even knowing that they were writing a book about marriage. The tears immediately started to fall and they grabbed my hand and prayed for me, for my husband and my family right then and there. Right there in the middle of the photoshoot we were praying and thanking God for restoration. They didn't ask for any details nor did they flinch when I told them why I was separated. Thanking God for clarity and transformation, like me, they too believed in marriage, but more importantly we all believed that God could change any situation. In that moment, they touched and agreed with me. Though the journey has been long and hard, God has restored my marriage and my family. As I write this forward, I stand as a true testimony to you that Marriage Can Win.

There are many to thank that helped me to stand during our journey of "becoming" restored. I thank the Hylick's, because they played such a crucial role in helping me continue with the breakthrough that started in the car. They helped the transformation in my mind match up to what I was feeling in my heart. Thank you Eric and Dr. Sykeisha for believing in marriage.

Contents

Introduction

Someone gets divorced every 10 to 13 seconds—in the time it took you to read to this point, someone got divorced. Surprisingly, those who marry when between the ages of 20 to 24, have the highest rate of divorce. You've probably heard people say that 50% of all marriages end in divorce, and this is an image that we are destined to help change. While this is somewhat accurate, it's also a bit misleading. As it turns out, studies also demonstrate that age can play a significant role in determining a marriage's fate. These couples are nearly twice as likely to get divorced as those who got married between the ages of 25 to 29 years old. The divorce rate is even higher for a third marriage it's a whopping 73%. It seems like when it comes to marriage, practice doesn't make perfect. That's why the divorce rate continues to get higher for each additional marriage. Nearly 3 out of 4 adults, on their third marriage end up divorced again. Nevada boasts the highest divorce rate. Maybe it's because of all the casinos, legal prostitution, or maybe it's because the desert is depressing. Whatever the reason, the fact is, Nevada holds the dubious distinction of the state with the highest divorce rate. Did you know that 9.1 per 1000 population get divorced? The State with the lowest divorce rate is Massachusetts at 2.1 per 1000 population. **When researching, we found that adults who didn't attend college and have a low household income are more likely to be divorced.** Non-college educated couples are nearly 20% more likely to get divorced within the first 10 years of marriage than college-educated couples. Lower-income marriages just tend to be more unstable. Christian couples have the same divorce rate as the national average. Arkansas has the highest rate of individuals married 3 or more times. Men and women in Arkansas are twice as likely to be married three or more times than the national average. The best guess as to why this is the case is because people tend to get married at a younger age in Arkansas.

Even though people are unsure on the basis of how these statistics are measured, we do know; marriages are more likely to last if you incorporate love, trust, forgiveness and respect and have a desire and a commitment to make it to work come hell or high water. Research has identified certain qualities associated with more stable marriages: **effective and consistent communication, conflict resolution, emotional support, dedication, and a willingness to sacrifice.** So if you know that some of these core concepts are not being incorporated into your marriage then we definitely want to connect with you.

We've been in your shoes before and we too were unsure as to how we were going to overcome the challenges of lack of time management, misdirected priorities, and feelings of isolation and rejection and generally being overwhelmed. The good news is that through all of the challenges, the ups and downs, one thing remained consistent is that we wanted our Marriage to Win and yours can too.

The word **WIN** means;" **to be successful or victorious in"**. We traditionally associate winning with events such as sports, debates, and various types of competition amongst a person or group of people. The act of winning must first be mentally realized before it becomes an action. In comparison, many people come into the covenant of marriage already defeated because they are focusing on what could go wrong. Before walking down the aisle, the focus is on planning the ceremony, the dress, the food, the guests, location and the reception. While all of that is great; the amount of time and money put into planning the wedding of our lives, could be put into the planning of a lifelong marriage.

What constitutes a lifelong marriage? Do you have a model by which to emulate? If you are anything like my husband or me, you had no idea or the model in which you had was not a positive one. We're here to teach you how to take what seems to be hard work and turn it into teamwork, dedication, and commitment. If you are reading this book, it is an indication that you are passionate about being victorious in your marriage. It signals that you are strategically positioning your marriage to overcome" The Great Divide ".

Before you begin, we want you to establish a winner's mindset by asking you to rate your answers to the following questions. **Using a scale of 1 to 5 (1 extremely unsatisfied, 2) somewhat unsatisfied, 3) satisfied, 4) somewhat satisfied, and 5) completely satisfied)**

How do you Rate your relationship in the following three areas?
1) Communication
2) Finances
3) Sex

How does your spouse rate your relationship in those 3 areas?

Where do you agree?
Where do you disagree?
What is your plan for dealing with challenges and disagreements?
What is your communication style?
Where and when do you want to discuss your issues?
Who handles the finances?

After reading this book and gaining an understanding, you and your spouse should answer the questions again. Compare your answers from before and witness the transformation of your understanding of how to help your marriage win!

Each chapter provides various points to ponder and practical application tips. We want to be sure that you're not only reading this information but applying each technique as it applies to you. Additionally, we've included real conversations with couples that have experienced marriage woes and what they did to correct them. These conversations are real, relevant, raw and radical. It is our hope that you and your spouse develop a greater desire and greater level of commitment to making the necessary adjustments so that you can have the transparent, candid conversations necessary to help your MARRIAGE WIN! We are rooting for you.

"A great marriage is not when the 'perfect couple' come together. It is when an imperfect couple learns to enjoy their differences. "

author - **Dave Meurer**

Chapter 1 - "Playing To Win"

The term" **win**" means to be **successful or victorious in a contest or conflict.** When two people become joined together as husband and wife at some point during their relationship, there will be conflict. The difference between those who win in their Marriage and those who don't is more often than not, their mindset. As a child one of the things that I noticed about my father was that he was extremely competitive this can be a very good characteristic to have, especially when you are competing against another person or people. He always wanted to be the best in everything that he did. This desire was a great characteristic to possess and was extremely beneficial when he served in the Army; however, it needed to be put into proper perspective. I noticed this same drive in my husband. I watched his old VHS tapes when he played football back in High School at Ft. Pierce Central. This drive and tenacity to win resulted in his being sought after to play football for some of the top Universities in the Country. What separated these two men in my life? Why one winning in marriage and the other is did not? Their mindset.

One of the key points that one needs to be mindful of is that winners need to be able to celebrate their victories as well as their defeats. If there is an area in which you are not winning, go back to the drawing board, look at where you need to make adjustments and redraw the plan. So many times I've seen people throw up their hands and say "I'm done with this!!!" When they are faced with an obstacle in their marriage instead of rolling up their sleeves figuring out where the problem lies and getting to work to make the necessary adjustments. Why is this the case? I mean we work hard on our jobs which in most cases is not a life time commitment. Why are we so easy to walk away from a marriage but will fight tooth and nail to keep a job, or get a promotion, or get a new house or car, or get our kids through school, but when it comes to our marriages we walk away?

While the exact words of a person's vows may differ most wedding vows. Most traditional vows are as follows:

"I,_____(husband's name), take you_____(wife's name) to be my wife, to **have and to hold from this day forward; for better or for worse; for richer, for poorer; in sickness and in health; to love and to cherish from this day forward until death do us part.**"

I also repeated those same vows demonstrating my level of commitment to the marriage. As we began to reflect over these vows, we had to think about our marriage and were we honoring the commitment that we had made as a couple, not once, not twice but three times. Yes, we were married to one another three times, but we'll discuss that topic later. I want you to take one moment and reflect on your wedding vows, even if the wording was not the same, the principle still stands. Utilize your name and your spouses name in the vows above then take a few moments to reflect. Are you actively engaging in the commitment to the vows that you stated above? If so, I applaud you, if not, **what's holding you back from doing so?**

Without pointing fingers at your spouse, like we often tend to, reflect on the ways in which you can and should make changes to honor the commitment that the two of you made. **Remember the two of you are on the same team.**

~ **Many marriages would be better if the husband and the wife clearly understood that they are on the same side.**

Zig Ziglar

Chapter 2- Complementing vs. Competing Against One Another

Another key point to be mindful of is that you and your spouse are on the same team. I have yet to see a team win the NBA Finals or a Super bowl by fighting against one another, but by operating strategically, **together** they become victorious.

Please don't get me wrong. If you have been divorced, we are not in any way, shape or form, here to judge you or make you feel condemned. Our sole purpose is to shed some light on an area in which we are extremely passionate about, which is winning in marriage.

Key Characteristics of a Couple who wins in Marriage

- They must be in constant **learning mode**. Marriage is a marathon not a sprint so the information that we learn about one another and the process of marriage takes place over time. Regardless of the phase that you are in your marriage, be it newlyweds, or have been together for decades, is essential to think of marriage as an ongoing class. In the healthcare arena, in order to maintain my license to practice, I have to maintain at least 30 hours of continuing education in order for my license to remain valid. That means I have to invest time to continuously learn about the changes that are constantly taking place in the healthcare arena, so I can me more informed and be better equipped to handle challenges when they come my way. This same concept applies to your marriage. Your spouse will grow and change over time, and you've made a commitment to learn about him or her and also teach your partner about you. This process is not an overnight occurrence. At the end of the continuing education training, there is a test that you must pass in order to demonstrate that you have grasped and are able to apply that information in your area of expertise. The same holds true for marriages. You will be "tested" aka "challenged" on the information or lack thereof. The true test comes in how you apply what you've learned.

A) A couple that does not give **up during times of persistent testing**. Over time, your spouse may surprise you often times in ways that delight you and sometimes in ways that frustrate you. It is imperative that the two of you find new ways to compromise and build your life together. In order to win in your marriage, it is essential that the two of you consider each triumph, as well as, each setback that you face to be an opportunity for learning and growth. When a couple utilizes this approach to challenges they are more likely than not, to have a positive outcome and are stronger for it. They are also more likely to persevere.

B) A couple who has a **pleasing attitude and personality**. In order to accomplish this task the couple has to develop a **winner's mentality**. One way in which to do this is to begin to replace the negative thoughts with positive ones. On a daily basis we encourage our children to verbalize at least 5 positive things about themselves before they go to school each day. We explain to them how important it is for them to set the tone for their day. This same concept holds true for our marriages. Begin to decree in your private time positive things about your spouse. Also begin to encourage and thank your spouse for their strengths. Whatever your focus more on tends to be what sticks in our minds. Our goals should be to build our spouses up and not tear them down for their shortcomings. We highly recommend incorporating positive affirmations into your morning routine to help you overcome any differences between the two of you.

A few examples of the affirmations that wives can declare daily over their husbands

- I accept him and love him for who he is
- Our relationship is becoming stronger each day
- I will begin to see things from his point of view and not just my own
- I will pay attention to his needs
- He walks daily in his purpose
- His gifts and talents are being revealed to him daily
- He walks boldly and confidently as a leader of this home
- He models positive behavior for our children daily
- He uses wisdom in prioritizing his day

And likewise the husband can do the same for his wife.

C) A couple who is in **control of their emotions**. Don't make permanent decisions in a temporary situation. Yes your spouse can have the innate ability to push that button that just makes you cringe. We encourage you to set boundaries. Have the conversation with your spouse that lets them know what your triggers are and agree together not to push those buttons. Agree on a safe word that you can use to signify that the discussion is becoming too intense and one or both of you need to take time out to cool down. Often times in the heat of the moment, tempers are flaring and before you know, you've said or done something that you regret. That momentary miscue can take time, weeks or even months for the other spouse to heal. Yes, words hurt, so choose them wisely. Instead of focusing on your weaknesses. Winners focus on their strengths

D) A couple that **focuses on each other's strengths**. Don't stay stuck in the same rut day after day. No person is perfect. Instead of focusing on your spouse's imperfections, learn to focus on their strengths. I am sure that as perfect as we all think that we are, there are things that each one of us needs to work on. I think that Dr. Phinehaus Kinuthia said it best when he said **"When you learn to celebrate SMALL victories, then you will gain the Courage to win HUGE Battles."** When was the last time you took a moment to celebrate a small victory in your marriage? Do you take the time out to acknowledge the one thing that your spouse did without your prompting them to do so.? We all love to be encouraged. When you focus more on the positive aspect of your marriage you tend to receive more positive and we know that the antithesis holds true. If you focus only on the negative, you tend to receive more negative. Set your marriage up to succeed by infusing your marriage with more positive words and words of encouragement that build each other up and not tear each other down.

Personal Testimony

I've often heard the saying, "you can't drive a car forward if you keep looking in the rear view mirror; eventually, you are going to crash." This quote stood out in my mind as I began to reflect upon a breach that occurred in our marriage. I'll be honest, it took me a moment to decide if I was going to walk in forgiveness or not. I realized that it was important to forgive myself. When the breach occurred in our marriage, I was hurt and my heart had been deeply wounded. I felt as if my heart had been ripped from my chest, deceived, pity, and at fault for what seemed to be my marriage failing.

Even though I was getting counseling and learning about how my past was now predicting my future, I still couldn't bring myself to forgive my husband. I talked to my pastor and she explained what I was going through; what was happening to my body physically and what was happening to me emotionally. I was shutting down again mentally. I would be at home trying to hold it all together for the kids and was failing miserably. I actually got to the point where I couldn't walk, speak, or eat anything; my entire body shut down. I was in complete physical shock. I never shared how I found out about his infidelity with anyone. I was intimidated, angry, and embarrassed. I found out on our way to church. I saw a text message that he had recently received and responded to it. Of course, I had a feeling that something wasn't right so I looked at it again, like. What? Are my eyes playing tricks on me? He knew because I wouldn't give his cell phone back to him. As the kids were in the back seat of the car, I just showed him the text message. I looked at him and said, "Really?" And of course he said, "What are you talking about?" I said, "Don't play with me. Read this text message!" I didn't want to alarm the kids by arguing so I left it alone. When we made it to church, I said, "Wait a minute, what's going on?" He's quiet all of a sudden. It felt awkward, he's looking at me and I'm looking at him waiting for an explanation. We proceeded to walk into the sanctuary like nothing ever happened. Now I'm faced with either sitting in my normal seat which is closer to the front of the church or sit in the back. I have never been one to run to the front row of church, but that morning, the usher escorted us directly to the front row. That was one Sunday in which the entire sermon was a big blur! I can only remember them singing the welcome song for all first time visitors and I wanted to run out of the door. My son was encouraging me to hug my husband and I was not about to let that happen!!! I didn't want it to seem obvious and the Pastor notice that something was wrong. It was just a challenge all around. But I am thankful that I had just taken a class on rejection and how to deal with it and it kind of gave me a little bit of an edge on calming down and thinking instead of reacting. It taught me to maintain my sanity throughout the entire situation because if not, I don't know what kind of situation I'd be in now. Six weeks of training on how to deal with rejection, low self-esteem, and how to deal with this type of situation made a big difference. But to be honest, my insides were messed up but on the outside I was unbothered.

With this series of events, it took a while for me to get back on track and go through the forgiveness process. A lot of people think that you can just go through that, forgive, forget and move forward; that's not the case. It's a long process within oneself; it really does impact you physically, emotionally, psychologically, and it takes a lot to rebuild mentally.

 As I began to meditate and seek out guidance from the bible, the answers would come to me through bible verses. **How could I expect to feel better if I couldn't forgive my husband as God has forgiven me?** As time went on, I began to heal, forgive, and ask for forgiveness. It sounds easier said than done, it was a struggle. Everytime I attempted to venture outside of forgiveness, my heartache started where it left off; it was as if somebody ripped the band aid off of an open wound. It would be at that point where I would have to start the healing process all over again. The process of starting over, made it even more painful and more challenging to heal because I would focus on all of the negative things. **I eventually got fed up and made the decision not to remain stuck and hold onto such negative emotions.** I needed to heal, not just for my children and for my marriage, but I needed to heal for me, so that I could be healthy and happy once again.

I was determined to get back to my happy self by engaging daily in prayer, open communication with my spouse and committing to forgive with an open heart. I had to recognize the triggers that would send me back to that place. We had to decide as a couple that we would set aside a time to discuss things whether good or bad, ask any and all questions pertaining to the situation without aggravating the other person with condescending remarks, and then we would move forward together with an agreement or compromise. We agreed that I would not constantly re-hash the past so that I could heal and that he would be sensitive and open when I had a challenging day. We were able to commit to communicating openly in order to solidify our future as a renewed married couple looking to enjoy life together no matter what problems may arise. It was at that point that I felt strongly about **forgiveness** being a part of helping other marriages to win.

Chapter 3 - Walking In Forgiveness

Physically, we may experience emotions such as fear, depression, frustration, anxiety, self-hatred, and loneliness. When we do not forgive someone, we tend to replay or relive that negative experience. We also tend to exhibit emotional symptoms such as anger, hatred, resentment, and may even desire to seek revenge. The inability to forgive your spouse can become a barrier between you and God. It stifles your prayer life and decreases your peace of mind. The Bible states in *Matthew 6:14-15,(NIV) "For if you forgive other people when they sin against you, your heavenly Father will also forgive you. But if you do not forgive others their sins, your Father will not forgive your sins."*

Now, I don't know about you but these days there are enough responsibilities that come along with marriage that I dare not add anything else to my plate that can hinder my connection with God. I am definitely not going to sugarcoat this subject because the fact remains that when a man and woman become joined together as husband and wife, you have two imperfect beings coming together who both have some degree of baggage brought along with them. Do you have a plan in place to operate in forgiveness when your spouse makes a choice that results in an offense to you? The reason I pose this question is because at some point in our marriages, our spouse's reactions to certain things may not be favorable.

It is essential for couples to maintain an open line of communication so that we can discuss these issues candidly and move forward without adding to our mental list and blowing up later.

I refer to the concept of "winning" regularly because I had to learn to **shift** my mindset from that of being defeated to one of becoming empowered. As parents, our children often make mistakes and what is our reaction most of the time? 99% of the time we are disappointed but we forgive and love them the same. While it is not without consequences, they were aware of why we were disappointed and how it made us feel, so why does this dynamic change when we are married? Chances are the child is going to make a mistake again but that doesn't mean that we shut down our dialogue with our kids or turn our backs on them. Instead, we come up with other methods or manners in which to help them understand why certain behaviors, attitudes, and bad decisions cause us to feel disappointed as parents. Why not extend that same courtesy to our spouse?

I know that you must be thinking well a child needs to be taught but my spouse should know. I agree to some extent that there are certain things a spouse should know, but the truth is that they may not know. Men and women have different love languages. What hurts and offends one spouse may not impact the other and vice -versa. But before you throw in the towel and assume that he/she just "don't get it", go back to the drawing board and begin to switch places with your spouse for a moment. Put yourself in their shoes for once. As human beings, we are all imperfect beings.

Why Should I Choose To Walk In Forgiveness?

Let's reflect for a moment. Have you ever said or done something that you know good and well should not have been said or done but you wanted your spouse to walk in forgiveness and understand it from your perspective? While constructive feedback is healthy in our relationships, too much can be very damaging. If you are constantly complaining or pointing out flaws in your partner's behavior, this can become a hindrance to your growth as a couple. This is why it's essential that we walk in forgiveness.

Forgiveness can be defined as "an intentional and voluntary process by which a person undergoes a change in feelings and attitude regarding an offense". Additionally, the person lets go of negative emotions such as; vengefulness, with an increased ability to wish the offender well.

Forgiveness is not to be misconstrued with any of the following:

Condoning; failing to see the action as wrong and in need of forgiveness
Excusing; not holding the offender as responsible for the action
Pardoning; granted by a representative of society, such as a judge
Forgetting; removing awareness of the offense from consciousness and reconciliation (restoration of a relationship).

Forgiveness is one of the most essential components to a successful marriage that can win. It is in these marriages that the husband and the wife are not only surviving marriage but they are in fact, thriving.

While the decision to forgive one's spouse for an act may occur quickly for some, the pathway to forgiveness is a process. For some couples, it may be relatively quick and for others it can be more challenging. Forgiveness is a process that will require dedication, focus, openness, and commitment from both parties. Forgiveness is not only for the spouse that committed such an offense; it is for the spouse that was offended as well. Did you know that harboring ill feelings and resentment towards your spouse can manifest physically, emotionally, and spiritually?

Forgiveness is a choice. One of the things about forgiveness is that one must be intentional when deciding to open your heart with acceptance to change. Every conversation that you have from that moment forward should not involve the past situations that you've already forgiven. You must move forward knowingly accepting that you can't change the past. There will be challenging days where you need to discuss something because it simply is unsettling. First, try writing it down (to free yourself of emotional bondage) and then after reading over, decide if it makes sense to involve your partner. I caution you, don't remain in that moment but try to come up with a presentable solution in order to tame tension. You miss out on so many other opportunities because of an inability to move forward if you choose not to process the situation.

"A good marriage is the union of two good forgivers."

— Ruth Bell Graham

Take 10 minutes of quiet time to reflect.

Points to Ponder:
1) Do you have a plan in place to handle the time when your spouse may say or do something that offends you?
a) If so, what is your plan?
b) If not, what strategies do you plan to utilize to handle the situation?
2) Are there any areas in your marriage in which you have not walked in forgiveness but you need to address? (If so, what's holding you back?)
3) What information have you gained from this teaching on forgiveness that you did not recognize before?
4) How do you plan to incorporate this into your marriage going forward so that it can win?

Scriptural References

Matthew 18:21-22: *At that point Peter got up the nerve to ask, "Master, how many times I forgive a brother or sister who hurts me? Seven?"*
22 Jesus replied, "Seven! Hardly. Try seventy times seven!"

This verse speaks to the magnitude by which we must be willing to forgive our spouses. Everytime he forgets to put down the toilet seat or leaves his clothes in the middle of the floor, or when she leaves the top off of the toothpaste, or forgets to mention the extra pair of shoes that appears on the credit card bill, you must plan to forgive these things. So when the more challenging issues arise, you'll be armed and ready to discuss and move forward with a clear conscious.

Matthew 6:14-15The Message (MSG)

"In prayer there is a connection between what God does and what you do. You can't get forgiveness from God, for instance, without also forgiving others. If you refuse to do your part you cut yourself off from God's part."

<u>Communication</u>

Research shows that an alarming 50 percent of all marriages in the U.S. results in divorce. Wow! Both my husband and I are products of twice divorced parents, which is why we're so passionate about helping marriages survive difficult times. We didn't want to become a part of the statistics; we decided to **take action**! It's important to be equipped with the tools necessary to help your marriage before it gets to the point of needing outside support. We have quick and easy access to manuals (both online and physical books) for getting our driver's licenses, birthing/raising children, and starting businesses. But why aren't we investing an equal amount of time in preparation for one of the biggest decisions in our life; getting married and maintaining those marriages?

Chapter 4 - Who or What Is Influencing Your Spouse?

Let's think about the impact of reality shows on marriages today. When I was growing up, we didn't have reality shows where they paint this picture of what marriage is. Today it's all about the perfect dress or amazing ring. Sure it's about what leads up to the wedding but they don't talk about the marriage and longevity. It's almost like the wedding ring is for rent. When things are not easy and are not going the way you imagined; when you can't pay the bills and things get tough, there's a perception that you can replace your spouse with someone else and get a better result. The fact is: when you find a replacement you're still going through the same process of getting to know that person. Why not spend your energy and precious time developing and working on your relationship now? Your time is valuable. It's a precious commodity that we can't get back. Why not pour some energy in the marriage first before you look for an out? Stop looking at the calendar waiting to say, okay, it's been 72 days and things aren't perfect; so long, bye-bye! It happens too often. Short-term celebrity marriages are a perfect example. The perfect wedding, the amazing honeymoon and then three or four months down the line, maybe even a year or two later they're like, "I'm done!" There is no dedication to making the marriage work.

Reality television shows have begun to water down the concept of marriage and portray it in a negative light. It's sad that by way of media coverage, we witness marriages ending in annulment, less than 90 days after vows are exchanged. What does that illustrate to our children? Media portrays the break-up of marriages as something that is supposed to be normal. We have come to the conclusion that whatever is portrayed in the household as your children grow up, will be detected in the outcome of their future relationships. That means you set the standard for your children. You create the blue print for them to emulate.

Growing up in two-parent homes, it's even harder to decipher. Like anything in life, you have to have the proper tools and strategies to be able to win. Without those marriage tools it will still be difficult, but not impossible, to succeed. Couples don't automatically come with tools to help them overcome conflict. They might not know how to find a resolution to get them through the chaos that inevitably comes in a long term relationship. People need tools and strategies to overcome the chaos.

Chapter 5 - Are you All In or Just Testing the Waters?

If we start a business, we pour our heart and energy into that business. We spend extra time at our job because we're working toward a promotion or a raise. But when it comes to marriage, people don't think it takes just as much commitment, time, and energy to excel. It does! At work, you state a goal and easily reach out for help when you need it. But with marriage issues: people become more concerned of what other people might think of them instead of being forthright and asking for help.

Have you ever gotten to a point where no matter what you do or how hard you try, things just don't seem to be getting any better? You've heard that phrase: It takes two to tango. If you've given all you've got, all you can do is stand. It really depends on the severity of the situation and only you know. Is abuse involved? Is adultery involved? Things of that nature must be considered. But if you move forward, can you walk in forgiveness? Does that person even want to be forgiven? Does that person want to continue in the marriage? Those are the candid conversations that must take place in order to ascertain what to do and figure out the next step.

If we're going to succeed in this challenging arena, we're going to have to do it the hard way. We're going to have to learn from our mistakes and find out what really works. Then we're going to have to stop doing the things that don't work and start doing more of the things that do.

There's a plethora of literature available that defines the reasons why many couples often end up in divorce court. We have narrowed our focus for this manual down to three main topics that can be considered **"The Great Divide"** amongst marriages:

- **Communication**
- **Finances**
- **Sex**

Effective communication is another essential ingredient for the survival of marriage. A lack of clear and consistent communication can prove to be detrimental. This can often result in frustration, anger, and resentment. A lack of communication is at the root of many serious marital problems.

Where Did That Come From?

Have you ever taken the time to review where you developed the patterns for communication in your relationships? More often than not you picked up some of these patterns from either of your parents. If you can, just try to recall how your parents interacted and if they still interact the same way. Were there any arguments? How did they interact with one another? Were they careful and considerate when interacting with one another? Did they demonstrate the ability to compromise or did they just argue back and forth? Or was there any form of communication? These were the initial lessons that established your expectation on how to interact in a marital relationship. Your parents may be the root of the learned behaviors that you demonstrate even now as an adult. You may feel it's okay to strike at someone verbally because, "He is picking a fight with me." You may be correct, but that person has the power to decide whether a fight actually occurs. That power rests with the responder.

As **Proverbs 15:1 says, "A gentle answer turns away wrath, but a harsh word stirs up anger."** Perhaps the most essential quality for good communication in any relationship, and especially in marriage, is to be a good listener. You don't have to participate in every disagreement. The key to winning is recognizing which discussions require a response and which one don't.

_____

_____

_____

_____

_____

Chapter 6 - Timing Is Everything

The book of Proverbs tells us, *"A man finds joy in giving an apt reply—and how good is a timely word!" (15:23).*

The majority of the time, we should be more strategic in the timing of our conversations.One effective tactic that we have found is to **simply ask our mate for their undivided attention.** I don't interrupt the Super Bowl or the NBA Finals to discuss topics that are not of the utmost importance and vice versa. Instead, we do the following:

- Make a list of **a maximum of three topics** that each of us feel need to be addressed
- We **schedule** the proper time to have a discussion
- Each person is allocated a predetermined amount of time that varies between **20-30 minute** intervals. We're able to discuss our concerns **without any interruptions**, but we must stick to the three topics at hand.
- We must also **provide specific examples** to illustrate why we feel this way
- **Specify** what we need from our partner in order to address our concerns.
- Afterwards, the other spouse is given the same set of guidelines along with their 20-30 minutes to communicate their concerns.
- **We take notes, implement, and execute** while supporting each other's solutions to rectify the situation.
- We **make it a point to always close out our discussions with planning out a date that doesn't include the**

business of the household. This is the healthiest way we found in moving forward in love.

Don't be afraid to communicate with your spouse what you want. Often times we encounter marriages that have drifted apart and are on the verge of divorce simply because their needs were not met

My question to you is; how can one expect their spouse to meet a need that has not been communicated?

Couples, who incorporate effective communication skills into their marriages, understand the importance of their feelings instead of using it to fuel their statements or filter their partner's words.

Emotions can cause lapses in judgment, so the best way to avoid this is by explaining to your partner where you're coming from rather than assuming they already know. Be clear in what you expect and provide solutions. If you're unsure of the solution, take time to yourself before presenting it to your spouse. When you make a greater effort to understand each other's perspectives, the less likely you are to get caught up in your own and forget to consider your partner's feelings. In other words, it's not about running away from your emotions but confronting them while alone. On the contrary, it's about recognizing how emotions play a role in your relationship and effectively articulating them to your spouse while being clear and concise.

As the receiver, reiterate to your spouse the importance of their approach, repeat what you heard and give them a chance to change or make you better understand what they're communicating, and let them know that you value what they said. Be honest and let them know that you need additional time to process it. Your partner will be more accepting because they will feel that you won't just tell them anything and that you really are taking what they said into consideration. This communication strategy gives your spouse the opportunity to clarify anything and make sure you are both on the same page. As a married couple, we learn about each other every day; everything we learn should be as humbling as the next experience.

Perhaps the **single biggest mistake** you can make if you want to have a good marriage is to **always try to be right** in your dealings with your spouse. Why is this so destructive? Most often, in order for you to be right, the other person must end up being wrong. Most people dislike having others make them feel wrong. They will resent you for this, and even if you win the argument or get your way, you'll pay a price later on. It's always wiser to allow your spouse to be right and have their way as much as possible. To some of us, that maybe hard but believe me, it's worth it! Obviously, you may not want to compromise on things that are extremely important to you, but 90% of the time, it will make very little difference, one way or the other.

Here's a quote from Ogden Nash (*reprinted from the June 1994 issue of Readers Digest, p.130*) that states this point very well:

> To keep your marriage brimming
> With love in the loving cup,
> Whenever you're wrong admit it,
> Whenever you're right, shut up!

Don't destroy your marriage by being selfish and trying to get your own way all of the time. Compromise! Think about your spouse's wants, needs, and desires as well. This will cause you both to be more in sync with what you desire in a marriage that is winning!

_____
_____
_____
_____
_____

Chapter 7 - Establishing Boundaries in Your Marriage

We can agree that when we had some challenges in our marriage, the one thing we did not want to do was involve our parents. Once you start inviting your parents into that situation they hold on to the issues and they hold on to those frustrations and resentment. You and your spouse are all lovey-dovey going forward but your parents still harbor that resentment. The biblical things are once you get married you must cling to your spouse. You leave your parents and cleave to your spouse. Your spouse has to become your number one priority. So, your parents should not be allowed to dictate the course of your marriage. They should not be influencing you in your marriage especially if they don't have a successful marriage. You cannot allow them to influence your marriage because your marriage will end up the same way theirs did. And as far as friends and family members the same principle holds true. It's the same thing. You have to keep them at a distance. Keep their opinions at a distance. You cannot go to them for advice in your relationship if things are going to be life altering. You have to go to your spouse and you have to develop that relationship with them. What you used to have with your family and friends, now your spouse is the one. When you get married your spouse is supposed to be your best friend - your confidant. We like to use this analogy. Your spouse is almost like the Holy Spirit. Obviously the Holy Spirit and your spouse are two separate things but you can always rely on the Holy Spirit. The Holy Spirit would never lead you astray because the Holy Spirit is the truth. But your spouse hopefully has the Holy Spirit in them. The bottom line is, you have to cling to your spouse. It's best to have a biblically God-filled marriage because you're both evenly yoked. And I always use the example of water and oil. If your spouse is saved and filled with the Holy Spirit they are filled with water, and you're saved and filled with the Holy Spirit you are filled with water. When you pour the two jars together into one empty jar, the water mixes together and becomes one. If your spouse is filled with the Holy Spirit and you're not, you are oil. There will be a temporary mix but an inevitable separation. You can be poured into the same jar but it's not going to mix. One is going to sit on top of the other and they're going to stay separate. That's not what a marriage is intended to be, because you are not unbalanced.

When you're already married the one that's filled with the Holy Spirit must pray and cover the one who is not filled with the Holy Spirit. In that case, you start off with a disadvantage but if you choose to marry the unsaved spouse, you are automatically aware this person is not saved and you're not equally balanced, so you're going to start out with conflict. It is imperative that you must continue to pray for that spouse so that they become saved but not try to change that person but allow God to change them. You're going to push them away if you continue to force them into changing. **You have to let God change their heart and their mind.** You may be the one who may draw them to Christ; draw them to become saved and that's because you live the biblically correct way.

Here's what can cause an issue especially if it's a woman that is saved and the man who isn't saved. You chose to go into that marriage. You must still be submissive to the unsaved man whether he chooses the right decisions or the wrong ones. You still have to be submissive to his ultimate decisions, and for the family. You can't be saved, take over and say you know what's best and try to override that unsaved man because that does not line up with the word. Once you do that and come to that situation you're automatically starting unbalanced. But what you can do is pray to God to touch that unsaved man to make the right decisions. And I'll give you an example with We had incidences where we disagreed and we were living in Palm Beach, Boynton Beach, Boca Raton and we just couldn't agree. And I just said, "You know what? You just need to go pray." And she was mad at me! At first she was offended. In her eyes, I was judging and belittling her, "What do you mean I got to go pray?" she said. But you know what? She did. And when she did, something miraculous began to happen! As she submitted herself and sought God for his intervention in our marriage, I looked around and God was penetrating my heart. My initial thought was, What was I doing that was so wrong? It made me step back and reflect on my contribution to the situation. Here I was, boasting to myself, Yeah God is going to fix her so we won't have this drama anymore, but the reality was, he began to fix me as well. My mindset began to shift when we made God an integral part of our marriage. Instead of asking God to fix her, I began to cry out to him, **What am I doing that's causing this conflict?** But what Sakeisha did was go directly to the source who could bring about a change my mindset and shift my thought pattern. Instead of complaining about me, she shifted into **praying for me** and asking for revelation. There were times in praying for me and found out that she was the issue; that she had to make some changes. But either way, the conflict got resolved because you go to the highest power that can make the change. So no matter what we say, whether we're right or wrong, it may escalate to the point where it pushes you further apart. In that case you have to go to the higher power. So in the case of the unsaved spouse, the saved one has to go to God. He can save that spouse. He can change that situation. That person may be adamant about doing things their way and doesn't want to hear anything else. You proceed to pray to God and then the next morning he apologizes, changes his mind, and does it your way. You would then be astonished because it wasn't anything you did even though you knew you were right. The more you press, **the more you're going to push apart.** But if you go to God, **God will change the situation for you**. That's the importance of having God in your marriage because He's the one you need to go to because when one's spouse is weak the other needs to be strong. The strong one knows to go to God to get help when they are having issues. But without God in that marriage, who can you go to?

In our situation, we consulted a trusted leader in our church. We have a pastor that we can confide in where everything is strictly confidential. We reached out to her to discuss the extent of our conflict and how we were open to receiving her guidance. She didn't sugar-coat anything for us. She was extremely supportive and unbiased, but she insisted on exploring both perspectives. From there we created and implemented a plan for both of us based on biblical principles.

34

One of the facilitators of the Marriage ministry at our home church gave such a profound   example that still resonates with me to this day. She indicated that often time's conflicts arise in marriages over something that's really important to one spouse and not significant to the other. She used the illustration of how primarily women like to keep things neat and orderly especially how we like the bedroom decorated and then your husband comes home and doesn't acknowledge it and messes up all that you put your effort into can cause the wife to feel un appreciated. Believe it or not, that was a source of conflict in our marriage. Her position was from a place of empowerment, **Do you want to be married and happy or do you want to be right?** Is it really worth it to have conflict and division in your home over something as trivial as lying on your comforter? You've made it look nice and inviting so when he wants to get comfortable in that bed, you chastise him for doing so. Look at the mixed signals that you're sending to your spouse. So stop and think about some of the things that we allow to become a source of conflict in our homes and in our marriages. Does it really make sense? Is it really worth the hassle? You have to pick and choose your battles wisely. Are you addressing the true issue or is there some underlying cause that has not been addressed that is really the source? That's something that resonated with me.

Have you ever had a situation in which you found it to be difficult to communicate a concern to your spouse, so you just sat on that feeling and even buried it deep in your subconscious or ignored it all together? Then all of a sudden you exploded on your spouse? Well we have all been there at some point in time. Then there was another situation where I felt it difficult to communicate. It was hard to deal with the magnitude of it, I recognized the situation and I went straight to our pastor. I went to someone that I felt was qualified to help my situation. I'm not going to blindly go to someone especially if they've never experienced that situation. How would they be qualified if they can only give me an opinion based on no experience? It's easier to approach someone familiar and unbiased in order to get advice on how they dealt with it.

Friend or Foe?

Another big issue in marriage is the acceptance of platonic friendships with the opposite sex. A couple should definitely discuss this before entertaining being in an exclusive relationship; well before marriage. Some husbands and wives leave that are accepting of these types of relationships but there are boundaries that must be established and maintained.

Chapter 8 - Red Flags

One of the red flags to be mindful of is the types of conversations that you have with this "friend" - . Just consider this. Is this the type of conversation that you can have in front of your spouse? Are you divulging information about your spouse to that person? If I can't have that conversation with that person in front of my spouse, or if it's something where my spouse wouldn't be welcome then that's a red flag. Most of the people that I work with or interact with, they know my spouse. I bring him by my job and they get to know him. They are very open with him because there is nothing to hide. If we're talking anything about work, he is welcome to be there and is cognizant of what's going on. A key indicator is that you're interacting with a person where your spouse isn't welcomed and / or the conversations are held with ulterior motives, it raises a red flag. In order to WIN in marriage trust is an integral key. Let's be mindful of if it's something like a project that you have to work together with, try to do it during work hours or make it so others are there with you. If it's a one-on-one situation, especially in a non-public situation, that can be a cause for concern if trust has been compromised. If there is a degree of attraction and alcohol is involved, that's a definite no. Do not put yourself into a compromising situation where something could happen. So you want to avoid those situations as much as possible. Avoid putting yourself in compromising situations that could jeopardize your marriage.

It's all about timing and when to use wisdom to bring those types of things up. When my spouse and I are out, you can tell when some women are just flirting with him and I look at him and he will politely excuse himself because we have that communication where I give him "that look" where he knows I don't think it's appropriate. He's an extremely outgoing and friendly person. Both of our personalities are outgoing but I know where to draw the line when it comes to people, and I know when to brush it off in a nice way and keep going. He's more of an extrovert and He'll just sit there and chat it up because that's the personality that he has but then you also have to understand that I'm the person that he's committed to spend the rest of his life with. Once he walks out of that situation he's coming home with me. So we have to make sure that our marriage is destined to win.

And as a woman you can just tell something is not right. So I'm looking across and I see this woman and I can just tell something's not right. So I don't know when she started talking to my husband or something just did not sit well with me. I got up and went over there. I talked to him and I told him he needed to go sit down and I'll stay here and get the food. But we had to have that line of communication and he was honest. He said, "Honey, yes, I was attracted to that woman," but you have to be mature enough for your spouse to have those conversations with you. If not, holding that entirely on the inside, hurts! And it would be unrealistic for me to think that nobody else in this world is attractive. Like Halle Berry would walk past my husband and he's not going to be attracted and say, "Wow, she's beautiful." Yes, she's beautiful but we're married. I'm not going to follow or stare her down. Okay, she's beautiful, you acknowledge that. Bounce your eyes. Look the other way. Don't put yourself in a predicament where it can cause issues in your marriage. But we had to have that level of communication where he could say someone was attractive - and I thought that that was unusual and uncomfortable. You have to allow your spouse to be honest and human. Now imagine if I'm at the point where I'm always up in his face accusing him of things? Is he going to be able to tell me that? I'm not saying go be attracted to other women - not at all, but if you see something going on, you let me know and be comfortable in expressing that. I'm going to pray with you and we're going to have some communication. We can say we don't like being in that situation and that's not cool. That's a red flag and I'm going in the other direction because I value my marriage. As a wife, I interact with a lot of different people on a daily, and in certain circumstances lots of famous people. But I treat them the same way I treat anybody else and I don't cross that line. For some people, when athletes come to their place of business they take pictures with them and stuff like that? For me it's like yes, this is my place of business; yes, this person walked through the door, but I'm not going to jump across the counter and say, "Hey, take a picture with me!" I'm not going to cross that line. But I'll text my husband and say, "Hey, guess who's here?" and that would be the end of it. I'm not going to cross that professional line. That's not my persona. And I'm up front and honest with him about that.

Communication should be the centerpiece in all aspects of marriage. When you decide to tell your spouse everything and not leave things out. You want to communicate with your spouse about the things you like, the things that you dislike, and the things you deem as appropriate and inappropriate. You want to definitely know about their past and present. Additionally, the conversation should take place regarding their plans for the future. If you don't tell your spouse about your past and it catches up with you, it may impact your future with them.

Points To Ponder:

1) Do I listen attentively when my spouse is speaking to me?
2) Am I fully engaged in the conversation?
3) Is my mind preoccupied with other issues and since my partner is telling me what I'm doing wrong, I want to take the platform and discuss the issues that I've had with them?
4) Do we have a solution once we are finishing up our discussions?
5) Are we angry?
6) Do I allow my spouse to speak instead of over talking them?
7) Do you comprehend clearly what you mate is saying? If not, how do you communicate this? Is it in a loving manner?

~The true measure of a married couple is not how happy they are when times are great, but rather how they stand together when facing challenging times.

— Author George & Yvonne Levy

Keeping the passion alive in a marriage is often easier said than done. However, the couples who have a true desire to win in marriage will make the time to cultivate and maintain a healthy and satisfying sexual relationship. These couples tend to foster an even greater connection with each other and are often times less likely to suffer from depression, heart problems and other health maladies, according to experts.

Chapter 9 - Let's Talk About Sex!!!

Sex is one of the Three Great Divisions in the marriages of today. Typically, you would think that sex is the least issue out of the great divide that causes issues in marriages; however, it goes hand and hand with communication and finances. So where do couples get their information regarding sex in the marriage? Is it from their **parents, friends, school, past experience(s), or religion?** Often times parents don't want you to have sex so they will tell you very little or no information about it. Friends may be just as misinformed as you or worse and the church may only briefly mention the spiritual aspect of it.

The question has been posed in regards to how the church could aid in this endeavor. In most instances many churches have a Marriage Ministry which fosters an environment for married couples to connect and interact with other couples. We have been very fortunate to participate in the Marriage Ministry at our local church and through this we have been afforded the opportunity to interact with other couples in numerous cost effective endeavors, such as bowling, Salsa dance classes, game nights, had dinner at various restaurants, hosted Valentine's Day dinner/ dancing event and even attended a local Weekend to Remember Marriage retreat. One of the phenomenal things about being a part of this group is that we worked together cohesively to educate other couples on topics such as Blended Families, Conflict Resolution, Communication, Sex & Intimacy, etc. **The sky** is the limit when it comes to marriage but are you willing to reach for it?

Sex should solely be with a man and a woman that are married. **So now how do we learn how to provide the needs and wants of our spouses?** There has to be communication about sex between the two individuals about becoming one in deep passion, desire and pleasure. If you don't know what brings your spouse pleasure, then how can you expect the experience to be a pleasurable one? It may result in a less then pleasurable experience for both you and your spouse, and could result in a level of pain or discomfort that leads to that spouse not wanting to have sex as frequently or stop all together.

These fundamentals mimic exactly what has been taught in our church's marriage ministry session. Contrary to popular belief women are not taught to be docile and fragile. We are taught to be bold, fight for our marriage and fight for our families. We can't do that by sitting back waiting for something to happen. You've said, "I do" so if you aren't, why aren't you? There's no regret the next morning. The two of you are married; being spontaneous only enhances the connection between the two of you. It brings about excitement and anticipation. **Don't you want your spouse to be excited about your romantic times together?**

Perhaps we worry about sexual communication because of the vast range of individual differences that exist with regard to being sexual and a tad bit selfish. We feel strongly about our own tastes; we sense that our spouse feels similarly about theirs—whatever they may be. We recognize that anything personal we say about sex has the potential to stir, scare, offend, and unsettle them. Worse still, we sense that saying the wrong thing about our own sexual tastes or assumptions has the potential to unmask us as foolish, ignorant, or inexperienced.

Chapter 10 - Sex vs. Intimacy?

Sex and intimacy are two different things. Often times in today's society there is no clear line defining the difference between the two. Yes, you can have one without the other. Traditionally, sex is between one husband and one wife ideally with the intention of procreation. However, these days it's primarily seen as a physical act, just a temporary sexual experience to satisfy a physical desire. Many people can engage in a sexual act with another person and have no level of connection with that person. Marriage Relationships that are founded simply on sex can eventually fade; then what's that spouse left with? They will continually search for something to fill that void because they feel as if they're missing out on something.

True intimacy involves an emotional connection and it may or may not involve intercourse. It does take time to establish a level of intimacy; it's not something that is established in just one night. Intimacy is a cohesive factor in building a strong foundation in a marriage relationship. Sex just isn't enough to build that strong foundation that a couple needs in order to survive the challenges, ups, and downs that they will experience in life. Do you realize that there are some couples that because of age, health and/or emotional condition may be unable to perform a sexual act? Amazingly, they've already achieved a level of intimacy with each other such that the marriage continued to thrive, while others may fizzle away or survive on a hope. A married couple that achieved a true level of intimacy has a strong emotional connection that in essence holds them together. Surely, sex between them can only serve to increase that connection and love that they already have.

Can a marriage survive without intimacy?

"A physical level of intimacy is only natural and is necessary between a couple, to show a level of comfort and affection. Sexual intimacy is one of the best ways to do it. You may express emotions verbally but nothing says it better than physical intimacy."

— Psychologist Dr. Sharita Shah

Marriage requires a degree of functionality and there are quantifiable aspects such as how much time you spend together and in that time; what you do together that makes you both happy. Intimacy connects a couple beyond the physical, cognitive, and emotional aspect of their marriage. It's an unspoken bond that connects a husband and wife. There are plenty of men who get along well with their partners but don't truly 'connect' with them. You could argue the fact that we've had generations of parents like that to make it work in spite of. Most regret this when things happen, such as illness, separation, infidelity, etc. When they reflect, most would say, "I wish I had known her/him better."

Without intimacy you can have a functional relationship that meets your needs on some levels but there is so much

more when there is a true level of intimacy. The Bible clearly states that *"it is not good for man to be alone"*.
Mental Vs Physical Stimulation

Mental aspect of sex also helps to prepare a couple for the physical aspect of a sex within the marriage. You have to prepare the mood for sex; there are a lot of things standing in the way (i.e. finances, careers, stress, family drama, etc.) but the things that stand in the way from getting in the mood are normal. Things like having bright lights on and the television blasting, phones ringing, or kids can dampen the mood. Instead, have a plan, get a quickie, or wait until bedtime. Prepare the mood by dimming the lights and putting on some slow romantic music. Complete a task that helps the spouse avoid having to do it. Setting the ambiance by eliminating those distractions will likely be the cause of a happy spouse. Take a hot bath together while massaging each other after a long day. Have a light dinner with chocolate covered strawberries, wine, or sparkling apple cider for as a cost efficient date night.

Men are physically stimulated and women are more emotional stimulated by affirmations, compliments, and thoughtful gestures. Be original stay in tune with what your spouse adores. For the men, produce a creative quixotic setting that includes putting on your favorite lingerie and sashay sexily to their favorite music. Make a romantic CD, Light candles, put on lingerie, your high heels, and become the exotic dancer of the night. Do something that makes you feel sexy and confident; create some mind blowing intimate sex that will have your husband smiling for days whenever he thinks about you.

Refraining from Sexual Punishment

Our relationship with our spouse is the most important relationship of our lives. It is the centerpiece around which everything else in our lives revolves. Or at least it should be. Our spouse's mood and our love relationship can delineate our happiness and well-being, our sense of security, and even our self-confidence and self-esteem. When things are going well with our beloved, life is generally good and comfortable. Even when other parts of our lives are difficult or challenging, having the loving support and presence of your partner make these challenges easier to tolerate and overcome. But when there is turmoil in the relationship, it infects not only the equanimity between our spouses, but also it disrupts our peace of mind, our self-confidence and the solidarity of the marriage.

The husband or wife should withhold sex because they are upset or angry. The Bible clearly speaks against withholding sex. Paul said that spouses have the responsibility to meet their spouse's needs–within reason. Marriage is about compromise.

1 Corinthians 7:2-5, states *"But because of [the temptation to participate in] sexual immorality, let each man have his own wife, and let each woman have her own husband. The husband must fulfill his [marital] duty to his wife [with good will and kindness], and likewise the wife to her husband. The wife does not have [exclusive] authority over her own body, but the husband shares with her; and likewise the husband does not have [exclusive] authority over his body, but the wife shares with him. Do not deprive each other [of marital rights], except perhaps by mutual consent for a time, so that you may devote yourselves [unhindered] to prayer, but come together again so that Satan will not tempt you [to sin] because of your lack of self-control."*

In essence neither the husband nor the wife has a right to deny sex with the other, except if they both make a mutual agreement to abstain for a specified period of time for prayer and fasting. This is usually a brief period of time. One of the key components in your marriage is communication. Simply put, Biblically, "A wife cannot flatly refuse her husband, she may only ask for a delay (a rain check) and then she needs to make good on that rain check as soon as possible.

Modesty

Modesty for a married woman means being pleasing to the eye without revealing so much that there is nothing left to the imagination. I am a proponent for looking good when you are with your husband. Any man who is passing by should not be able to see exactly what's meant for your husband's eyes only. I believe strongly, that most men desire a lady in public and a freak behind closed doors.

We believe that there must be a degree of balance in every situation. I don't feel that the wife should walk around in granny panties, bonnets, and rollers when he comes home. He should see what he's been missing all day and remember why he chose you as his one and only. It doesn't mean that you have to look like a runway model all of the time but looking classy while sexy doing the dishes always wins! Men are physical but fragrance draws him in every time, greet him but make sure your personal hygiene is not be questionable. Comb your hair, brush your teeth, put on some good smelling perfume, and from time to time greet him in something sexy at the door.

Single "good girls" looking to be married can be sexy and classy at the same time. You don't have to be married to take good care of yourself. You should always strive to look your best when out in public. Being a Proverbs 31 woman refers to all of the attributes that a woman can possess, not just the external appearance. Act like a lady at all times.

Often time's couples will find themselves in the midst of a rut. They wake up at a certain time, go to work, they come home take care of the household responsibilities, including the kids if there are any, then go to bed and wake up and do it all over again. There is no variation, no spontaneity. We tend to become complacent in where we are. After a period of time, this can become monotonous.

Let's explore some scenarios that reflect some of the challenges that a few married couples have faced

- Tom and Sue abstain from sex until they got married and on their honeymoon it was painful and awkward for her. They didn't talk about it before getting married and they didn't talk about it afterwards. He thinks it is just great. Time goes by and she associates sex with pain and it happens less frequently until it just stops all together. Now the couple stays together but the marriage is cold and lacks intimacy altogether. They eventually have resorted to sleeping in separate rooms.

50

- Joe and Jill get married; Jill experienced pain and was not satisfied at all during intercourse, and she never sought out counseling or medical attention. She had been raped as an adolescent. Two years later Jill does not desire her husband and became curious, interested, and wanting a woman's intimacy. This is not an indication that we agree with this; however, this is a challenge that many couples are facing today.
- John climaxes too early and leaves his wife dissatisfied and beyond frustrated. A couple of years later she is having an affair with another man who satisfies her sexually.

There are many scenarios of issues with sex and intimacy that can happen and several reasons why a couple's sex life may not be as pleasurable. The three main reasons are:

1) **Frigidity**
2) **Guilt Factor**
3) **Fear Factor**

Frigidity aka" not wanting to have sex: not enjoying sex "is something that hits close to home with us. As a young girl, my wife was molested by her next door neighbor's grandfather. That was something that my wife kept to herself well into her adult life. Often time's women that are victims of molestation may become even more promiscuous. The opposite held true for my wife. She became more introverted and withdrawn. Subconsciously she began to develop a brick wall as a means to protect herself from becoming hurt and/ or violated again. **What does this have to do with sex and marriage?** I'm glad that you asked

Personal Testimony

We dated for four years prior to getting married and she always was a bit guarded. I assumed that was something that would change after marriage; however, as amazing as she is, it was a huge hurdle to overcome in order to win in our marriage. It took quite a bit of coaxing to get her to adjust to the fact that, not only is it great to have sex during marriage, but you should enjoy it as well. There is nothing sinful or dirty about sex between a husband and wife. We were created to enjoy each other's bodies. There was no reason for her to be inhibited from expressing herself sexually with me as her husband. I am sure that many husbands' out there can agree with me that it is necessary to get to the root of the cause of your wife being a **"Frigid Fannie"**.

Many wives may be accustomed to their husband being the initiator but truth be told, men love to feel desired by their wives. What man doesn't want his wife to seduce him and confirm that she still desires him and finds him attractive? Men are sight stimulated so why not give him something to be stimulated about? As I mentioned that most men want a lady in public and a freak in the sheets. They want to know that they are pleasing you and you enjoy sex with them. You can't expect him to just know, you have got to show him. Not just with your words, but follow it up with actions. You don't want him staring at the Victoria Secrets catalog; you should be his Victoria Secrets model. Yes we are fully aware that our bodies may change after a few years of being married but you should remind your spouse that they have a great catch. No one should be more attentive to your spouse's needs than you are.

Here is where learning about what pleases each other sexually can help promote a healthy, happy, and sexual marital relationship. The best foundation is for each person to experience deep passionate, pleasurable intimacy, and oneness. Each person is going to be different and what works for you may not work for your spouse and vice versa. For example, you may like to be kissed on your ears but your spouse is not turned on if it's done in return. God made each man and woman unique with different needs; pleasures and different erogenous zones are heightened differently. **You must communicate your desires in order to help your spouse understand what you like and dislike. If something feels good let them know, if it is not pleasurable, communicate that to them.** Learning to be sexually pleasing to each other has to involve truthful verbal communication and not just what you think they want to hear. Speaking candidly about sex would make our lives better, healthier, and happier

Another potential cause for a lack of sex in the marriage is the **Guilt Factor.** Women are commonly raised to believe that sex is forbidden. That engaging in sex deems one to be "a bad girl". After doing lots of research I found that certain cultures actually prepare their daughters for sex in marriage by encouraging them to meet the needs of their husbands sexually. Women tend to be more emotional beings and tend to hold on to things like guilt for a longer period of time than men.

The third most common reason for a lack of pleasurable sex within the marriage is the **Fear of Failure and/ or Rejection Factor.** This fear can be due to insecurity about previous physical and/ or emotional injury. Let's be real.

The majority of couples that are married today did not wait until getting married before having sex. Those past sexual experiences can shape or impact the way that your spouse views sex. The husband must be sure that he is not rough and insensitive to his wife's sexual needs. Additionally, some women tend to become fearful when it comes to sex because they fear rejection or being compared to another person sexually. It is imperative that one spouse is not critical of the other spouse's performance. Society has already created a stigma of how a woman's body is" supposed to look". Truth be told this can be a hindrance in the bedroom because one or both spouses are insecure about their appearance physically and their performance sexually. As women it is our sincere desire to be physically appealing and sexually stimulating for our husbands. I am reminded of an interview that we had with one particular husband, I'll refer to him as JT. His thought pattern as a man was entirely different. He said *"Look, when it comes to sex with my wife, I 'm not turning down anything, but my collar!"* It was his sincere desire to enjoy his wife's body, imperfections and all. Another husband shared with us candidly that his wife admitted that she had become insecure about her body because she had gained some weight over the course of their marriage and the birth of their children, while her husband had remained slim and trim. She even commented that she might feel a little more comfortable if he had gained a little weight as well. Many women share the same concerns for their body images if you want to win focus on what your spouse did that you enjoyed. Encourage them to continue. Additionally, you can tell your spouse which positions may not have been as pleasurable. Remember that timing is everything. Now you're ready to explore.

The Exploration Process

Take time to explore your body with your spouse:

Start with the toes and feet. Touch, kiss, and lick different parts and ask if it feels pleasing to your spouse. Take mental notes if you have to; most of all, relax. Work your way up from the bottom to the top and vice versa.

For the woman, explore her body again touching, kissing, and licking the different areas of it Pay close attention to the areas which brings her pleasure? Ask her what she likes as you explore her vagina with your hands lips, tongue, fingers, and mouth. There are a couple of spots that may be more pleasurable than others. Pay attention to her body reaction. Your goal is to find the spot that is most pleasurable to her. The Ultimate goal should be to reach the "G Spot". There are a couple of spots that may be more pleasurable then others. The clitoris is very sensitive and erogenous. When touched, kiss or licked it can bring great pleasure to the woman. Also you can insert your finger inside the opening of the vagina and press on the vaginal wall and move slowly around the wall stroking at every point taking notice of the points that bring her pleasure. Keep going to find the most sensitive spot referred as the G- spot area. Press and tap toward the front of the vagina toward the pubic bone upwards. Your goal is to find the spot that is most pleasurable to her.

As for the wife, start off by kissing his neck, kiss and nibble on his nipples, work your way downward. Men, guide your wife's hand and tell her what you like best (or moan a little); how hard, how soft, how fast or slow and the best locations for her touch. The most sensitive part of the penis is the head and that is where you focus most of your attention. Again try the touch, kiss and licking to find the optimal pleasure points.

Explore different positions and techniques, if your spouse likes a certain position better than others then give them what they want. If you spend your time and effort pleasing her and she spends her time and effort pleasing you then you have overcome majority of the issues in the marriage. Take time out afterwards or the next day to reiterate how good it was. When flirting, give hints to your spouse on what you look forward to them doing to you and what you look forward to doing to them. Always keep it hot in your bedroom. Know what your partner looks forward and introduce new things that you think they'd like.

Spice Up Your Bedroom Activities

Here are some popular positions to try if you haven't already tried them and challenge yourselves in creating something different. Make your own little sex manual. Be creative make it fun. Be mindful that this is a process and one partner may be more experienced than the other so patience is key. Your assignment is to have a candid conversation with your spouse and openly discuss which of these activities the two of you would like to try. The two of you may commit to trying one new position per week.

Flatiron
- **How**? You lie face down on the bed, legs straight, hips slightly raised.
- **Benefits** associated with this position is that shallow thrusts and deep breathing will help him last longer thus enhancing pleasure.

G-Whiz
- **How?** You lie back with your legs resting on each of his shoulders.
- Benefit is that it narrows the vagina and helps target your   G-spot

Face-off
- **How?** He sits on a chair or the edge of the bed; you face him, seated on his lap.
- Benefit is that it allows the wife to be in control of the angle and depth of the entry and thrust.

Cowgirl

- **How?** You kneel on top of him, pushing off his chest and sliding up and down his thighs.
- Benefit is that the woman can relieve some of her weight from his pelvis by leaning back and supporting yourself on his thighs.
- Bonus you'll delay his climax and intensify yours.

The positions above are just a few of the numerous positions that you and your spouse can incorporate into your sex life to keep it fresh and exciting. The two of you can be creative, find different places as well, try different locations throughout your home, and change the atmosphere in your bedroom or living room, if you don't have the finances to take a vacation to the beach, transform your home into your own private oasis. The two of you can meet somewhere secluded. Have a brief interlude during your lunch break. We do encourage you to use wisdom in your choice of location.

Chapter 11 - What's Your Back Up Plan?

Studies have shown that disagreements between married couples about money tend to have a significant impact on the alarming increase in the number of divorces in America today. In fact, couples tend to fight about money twice as much as they fight about other topics. Like many other married couples today, Eric and I were not immune to the "money fights". In fact we didn't realize just how differently we saw money until we had to file for bankruptcy on Christmas Eve about 7 years ago.

Can I share with you how heartbroken, I was that year? It was the first time that I realized that unless we made some drastic changes in the way that we saw money and in our spending habits, we were going to have difficulty rebounding from this. One hint of encouragement that I do offer to couples that are or have faced bankruptcy, foreclosure, repossession, is that it is not the end of the world. Your marriage is not over. Reflect upon those wedding vows. "…. In sickness and in health, for richer or for poorer, till death do us part."

Now is the time to shift your mindset to a winner's mentality. Our relationship is even stronger financially after Bankruptcy than it was before. How is that? I am glad that you asked. First, after bankruptcy we realized that we had to go through a maturation process. We began to see how essential it was to have a plan for our finances both long term and short term. Unfortunately, many couples don't consider the unexpected loss of income, illness, or things of that nature that may impact one's ability to thrive financially. We never planned on a job loss or a three-year period living on one income. We never envisioned going through phases in which we had lights disconnected and having to tell our kids that we were staying in a hotel for a quick "vacation" because our lights had been turned off.

It's easy to have a great relationship when all of the bills are paid but the true test came when our accounts were all negative out. We were living like we had an unlimited supply of finances but when all you have is each other, what's your plan?

You must communicate about your finances. Whether you're just starting out or have a long term relationship, you must communicate your future goals: a year from now; five years from now; ten years from now. Be specific in those goals. It's vital to have a specific plan in place in how each of you plan to obtain those goals.

If you're looking to get married and your partner states their goal is to become a team leader or on the management tract but you're looking to pursue higher education and become the director or CEO of a company, then that's fine. The goals are a little different there has to be a plan for your finances moving forward. You want kids, own a home, and drive a decent car. Okay. Make a plan. What can you expect right now and what do you expect to obtain in the years to come? You cannot expect to live in a 6,000 sq. ft. home and drive an expensive car when your goal is to accomplish this do not match up with this level of living. How many children do you want to have? Two, three, or even perhaps four children??? You have to communicate those things. Will you be able to provide the basic necessities for the children such as food, clothing and shelter? Provisions need to be made for their education.   As a couple you need to look at your current housing situation and ascertain if it the atmosphere there is conducive for raising children or will it require you to relocate.   That's all a part of communicating with each other and making a plan. Where do you want to be a year from now, or five years from now and even ten years from now?   It's imperative that you establish a plan and delineate those things that are necessary to make it happen.

Once you get married the challenging part is often" how to stay married". The same amount of creativity that we utilized during the dating phase must still be incorporated into our marriages on a regular basis. Do you recall when you two were dating, what were your weekends like? How often did you date? What did you do during your date s? Jazz, concerts, walks in the park, or trips to the beach? Last minute weekend getaways are spontaneous and essential to the life of the marriage. I can recall when my husband and I were in college and neither of us had any significant income, we were super creative. Money never really was an option because we found a way to work with what we had. Our primary concern was just being together and spending much needed quality time. We could drive to the park in Tallahassee, walk around the lake, and spend countless hours talking about our hopes and dreams. We would literally talk until 2 or 3 o'clock in the morning. We never ran out of things to discuss. In those rare moments of silence, we would simply gaze into each other's eyes and hold each other. Other times we would jump in the car and drive 3 hours away to Ft Lauderdale/Miami or take in a comedy show in West Palm Beach. We made it happen on a budget and out of love, we created the elixir to happiness.

We understand that you have bills to pay, jobs, and life's stressors, but rest assured, investing in a weekend trip out of town is a whole heck of a lot cheaper than a divorce lawyer, RIGHT? If you're not able to splurge on a weekend getaway, hire a babysitter, or have a relative watch your kids for a weekend, and transform your home into a romantic retreat. If you've always wanted to visit Hawaii, decorate your home, especially your bedroom, into an oasis. You can find inexpensive décor from Wal-Mart, Dollar Tree, and Target, etc. Be creative within your budget and see a romantic escape in your near future. You will definitely be pleased with the return on your investment. (Smile)

When it comes to the great divide for marriages, finances rank among the highest of the top three. When the bills come in and money goes out the stress levels tend to increase. The sex goes down and tempers rise dramatically. Wives need to feel safe and secure and confident that the needs of the family will be met. Men have a sense of accomplishment when they are able to provide for their family. Men are protectors by nature. When this does not occur, a few things can happen; the husband begins to question his ability as a provider for the home and for his family, subsequently his self-esteem can decrease. Men that have issues with their self-esteem may resort to or may become engaged in behaviors that can be destructive to the marriage because his desire is to find something to take his mind off of the situation and find a solution to make him feel better about himself.

Each man is going to vary in the path that he chooses to take in order to fill the void. While communication with your spouse is the ideal manner in which to handle these situations, these men may find themselves, **spending excessive amounts of time playing video games, spending unnecessary money, watching television, spending less time at home, increased consumption of alcohol and /or illicit drugs**, or the new thing; social networking.

Sounds familiar?

It's going to be challenging because you have two individuals coming together from two different backgrounds and a history of experiences with different perspectives on the relationship. Now add the maturity level. One person is bound to be more mature than the other. It's really learning to come together with those strengths and weaknesses to learn to play together like a team. Sometimes it takes a while for a team to come together and learn to play but when they do they win. It's the same thing with a marriage.

It's a balancing act. One member may have strengths but it offsets the other one's weaknesses and helps build them up, and vice versa. That helps. In our example, I wasn't strong in finances but Eric was and he handled them. But in the process he taught me how to strengthen my skills so I was equipped to handle it when he couldn't. I was able to step up to the plate and take care of what needed to be done to support the marriage. Yes, it's natural to have those roles but do you understand it? Do you know why it works and what's going on? You need to take the time to communicate with each other so everyone is on the same page. These are the expectations because if he can't do it and I'm not prepared, then things can fall apart. But if you build that foundation and the storm comes you will be able to withstand it and handle the situation.

For example, there was an instance when I worked in a corporate office where one of my co-workers insisted on a vehicle that he wanted. He felt like he worked hard and deserved to treat himself. This is how he rationalized it. But his wife was focused on their finances, the lack of savings and it felt like it was going against their original plan. She was at a point of where it could have led to a divorce with the mental strain and breakdown.

As a visionary for the family a man should recognize his strengths as well as the areas in which he needs help. If he **knows that his** wife is more adept at handling the family's finances, that task should be delegated to her with the understanding that the two of them should be meet a minimum of once a month, preferably before the month starts to lay out a strategic plan for the family's finances for the month.

As a wife who oversees the finances, you want to be mindful and not to cause division in your marriage over material things. What do you mean by this you may be wondering? We've often heard the common source of conflict in marriages about women and shoes or purses or men and cars or electronics. Don't throw away your marriage over a car, or a pair of shoes. Consider the big picture. Prior to buying a new car consider these things. Is this purchase going to affect our ability to meet the basic necessities of my family? What kind of impact will this have on our mandatory obligations? Will we still be able to pay the mortgage, utilities and provide food? While transportation is important, does it have to be the most expensive car? Is it something that we can plan for in the future?   Is there a way to pay down one bill to accommodate a new car payment?   Is this something that needs to happen right now or can it put off another six months to a year?   Present viable options for a win-win situation and communicate them with each other.

The average American couple is living pay-check to paycheck. In most instances this is a direct result of the unwise choices that we have made.   I think that **Dave Ramsey** said it best *""We buy things we don't need with money we don't have to impress people we don't like."* Now, our question to you is, How wise is that?

The Bible says that a wise man leaves an inheritance for his children's children. We often choose to invest our finances in a thing that bring about a temporary satisfaction but are it really worth it? Take a step back from your current financial situation and seriously evaluate if you are where you want to be financially. If you are among the group of Americans living from paycheck to paycheck consider this quote by Dave Ramsey **"You must gain control over your money or the lack of it will forever control you."**   Now we don't know about you but we're confident that if you are reading this book then you have a strong desire to bring about a change in your   finances   in   your   marriage.

Every situation is different but it's important that the couple come to some form of agreement and stick through it. The lesson here is experience. You don't give up on the spouse or the marriage because of a car but you do surrender to the process and trust that the experience will reveal what is meant to be.

From a spiritual aspect, the majority of most marriages create their own problems and they have to rely on the Father to bring them through, but once they overcome those obstacles they know it's because of the Father that they came through and they both mature as individuals and together as one in a marriage. You still have to stick it out with that spouse because the maturity level and past experiences will dictate how a person acts or reacts. So you have to be patient and show them love because that will overcome anything. There is a realization that they have overcome the obstacles and the pain together; they stood strong. That's when the maturity level of that marriage has graduated. Think about it. If their relationship was never tested, how would they ever know the depth of what they can do together? If there are always good times, you will never know the strength of true love because it's never been tested. You know there is resiliency. These are things that challenge you to grow. Of course, no one wants to be tested and you try to avoid that if you can. Ultimately everything won't be avoidable but when it gets to a point where you aren't in control, it's important to withstand the test. The foundation has to be solid.

It's going to be challenging because you have two individuals coming together from two different backgrounds and a history of experiences with different perspectives on the relationship. Now add the maturity level. One person is bound to be more mature than the other. It's really learning to come together with those strengths and weaknesses to learn to play together like a team. Sometimes it takes a while for a team to come together and learn to play but when they do, they win. It's the same thing with a marriage.

The two of you have to learn to operate together as a team. You must find your strengths and that complement each other. Each member of the team has a role and their responsibilities. . Biblically, the man is the head of the household and the woman is submissive to the man but it's taken out of context a lot. It does not mean he dictates everything. He's the one accountable to God. So when something goes wrong, God looks at him for what goes wrong in the household. But the expectations have to be established. That is not always easy because of our past experiences. These days, one spouse may come from a one parent household where it's just the mother - or even if there are two, the mother may very well be the dominant figure and that's all that spouses sees and therefore that's the pattern that they emulate.

There will be differences and it will require an adjustment on behalf of both parties. And no one knows how long that adjustment period is going to be but it's essential to have those pieces of the puzzle mapped out in order to win. As a couple you have to figure this out together.

Before You Said I Do

Do you remember in the beginning when you walked down the aisle and said "I do"? The famous words you and your spouse repeated one after the other, "I will love, honor, respect, cherish, obey, for richer or for poorer, and thru sickness and health till death do us part". Translation: no money, no honey. Why? The couple neglected to talk about the combining of finances before-hand. Before marriage, the couple must come up with a plan in order to become one: that includes your short term and long term financial goals, the kind of lifestyle you want to live, addition of children, the purchasing of property, and credit scores. You have to come up with a budget and a plan to obtain the level of wealth that you desire. When it comes to the financial status of many couples today we have to ask ourselves, did we have the necessary conversations to establish goals for us individually and as a couple?

Did you discuss finances before or after marriage?
If so, where are you in your quest to obtain these goals? If not, what's stopping you?

It's not too late to get your family on track financially. Look for a financial advisor, schedule a time to meet with your spouse, and ask the necessary questions to ascertain his/her plans for your future. Decide if meeting with a financial advisor necessary.

_____

_____

_____

_____

_____

Points to Ponder:

- Do you have a job? If so, how much money do you make?
- What type of career do want to pursue and how do you plan to achieve it?
- What is your credit score? Do you have any money saved or are you planning to start saving money?
- Do you have life insurance for your family? Do you have medical, dental insurance (benefits)?
- Do you want children? If so, how many and do you have a plan for their educational needs?
- Do you have any current children, How many? If so, are you paying child support?
- Do you want to rent or own a home? Do you want to take vacations?
- Do you have cars? How much is your car payment?

These are some of the topics that should have been discussed prior to marriage. If you are already married and have not had these conversations, we have good news for you, it's not too late! Schedule some time **now** to have this discussion.   Pull out your playbook and make plans to win by sitting down with your spouse and get all of their bills, expense lists, and income statements to take a true look at the numbers. While establishing a budget may be the last thing on your mind; it is budgeting that keeps finances from going astray.

Making the Necessary Adjustments

Many couples make a mountain out of a molehill when it comes to finances; it's not rocket science, it doesn't require a lot to achieve positive results. It is as easy as grabbing a pen, paper, a calculator, a positive attitude, and a desire to get your family on track to financial freedom. Yes! There will be challenges along the way, but that doesn't mean that you give up.

For instance,

- List all the income for the month
- List all expenses the family spends in a month for (Specifically housing, utilities, food, entertainment, education, transportation, card bills, medical bills)
- Include daily expenditures such as, coffee run to Starbucks, haircuts, nail salon visits, after school activities for kids, snacks, and lunch
- Commit to tracking all expenses for all family members for at least 30 days.

In this age of technology, there are real-time budgeting apps on your smart phones and or worksheets available online to help get you started, free of charge!

More often than not there are expenditures that pertain to wants instead of needs and families choose not to cut down for convenience reasons. But when money is tight and the family is barely surviving paycheck to paycheck, it's time to take out the red pen and slash expenses. As a couple you need to decide what's deemed as an urgency versus something that can wait.

For example, the average household has cable; cutting out cable for six months can save a family on average somewhere between $600-$800/year depending on your service provider. There are numerous alternatives such as free movies from the local library, family game nights, or inexpensive hobbies.

As you deduct the savings from the cuts you make, add it to your bottom line on your budgeting worksheet. These additional savings could be transferred to eliminate or reduce credit card debt.

Establish Pre-Set Spending Limits:

- Couples should decide together the maximum amount each should spend without their spouse providing their input
- Include school aged children in in the discussion of basic family finances. Often time's parents may find themselves utilizing money to finance kids' needs and wants without regard for the family finances and these little expenses begin to accumulate over a period of time. When there is no set allowance amount, discuss it as a couple
- Implement creative ways for kids to earn their own spending money by taking out the trash, washing dishes and completing various tasks to help generate income. This should be included in the budget

My wife and I decided that it was time for our daughter to gain firsthand experience with earning money. Once my 13-year-old began to earn money babysitting; her decision regarding spending money changed drastically.

Creating Short & Long Term Goals

Have a family discussion about financial goals and how to reach them. Recognize that your family goals may not be identical to the couple next door, or even that of your father and mother. It is essential that you document your goals in writing so that you can see clearly the vision for your family. This also ensures that each spouse is on the same page financially. Also, be specific in regards to the time frame in which you want to accomplish each goal. Decide specifically who will be responsible for paying the bills. This can be challenging because many households may feel that the husband should be responsible for the finances. In marriage you need to recognize the strengths of each person. The wife may be stronger at organizing and keeping up paying bills in a timely fashion. If that is the case, delegate that task to her and the two of you can schedule a meeting monthly to discuss what bills need to be paid, the payment schedule, and the bill amount. After then, figure out what's left, what should be saved, and what should be put to the side for extracurricular activities.

Short Term vs Long Term Goals

What are our short term goals financially?
- Pay off Credit Card Debt
- Create an emergency fund of X dollars
- Pay off car note

What are our long term goals financially?
- Saving for college for kids
- Paying off mortgage
- Building a savings account of x amount of dollars
- Accumulating x amount in your 401k fund

To recap: communication comes first. It's better to initiate these conversations to ask each other what's important and talk about our dreams; to look at our finances and ultimately plan and take into account his dreams, her dreams, and communicate a unified plan and navigate that together. Compromise is extremely important but equally so is keeping that win-win mentality so it doesn't become a competition - a sort of his or hers - what I want versus what you want; to compromise through those obstacles and paint a full picture. But if one spouse decides to move forward with a financial decision against the will of the other then you need to surrender to the process.

Chapter 12 - Moving Forward

Once the most challenging hurdles have been overcome and the family has a better understanding of their financial situation, it is most important to keep moving forward and be proactive about finances. Thanks to technology today, there are many online money management programs designed to assist families in these endeavors. Did you know that you can input and track any expenditure utilizing various online resources?

Getting back in control of your family's finances will also help alleviate family financial stressors, renew your confidence, and can even help create new ideas to generate additional income. If you are still in need of assistance or desire a new job with better pay, don't allow things such as pride or fear to hinder you from trying to get back in good financial health.

The initial task of getting your finances on track is usually the most overwhelming portion of this equation. However, facing it head on is the only way to regain control of your family's finances. Otherwise, you are at risk for an unhealthy financial life for your entire family and a face a continuous struggle to make ends meet.

Zig Ziglar summed it up best when he said

"If standard of living is your major objective, quality of life almost never improves, but if quality of life is your number one objective, your standard of living almost always improves."

Chapter 13 - Submission Is Not A Curse Word

What does the true picture of submission look like for husbands and wives?

What does the word "submission" really mean? God's ideal is for a husband and wife to have a harmonious, loving relationship where each partner serves and prefers the other. In some people's opinion submission is seen as weakness; however, I believe the exact antithesis to be true. Submission comes from a place of strength. It takes a really, secure and mature person to willingly and graciously submit to their spouse.

At the beginning of our marriage I was vehemently opposed to the term submission. I mean at our wedding when my husband's best friend toasted us and referenced the following scripture on submission. I was smiling on the outside but I could feel my skin cringing underneath. It took everything in me to keep from screaming. I was raised by my father and believed that the only thing that I was to submit to my husband; was a receipt which is the exact opposite of what the Word of God teaches us; **Ephesians 5:22**, which tells wives to submit to their husbands.

One example comes from Sakeisha's personal experience. My parents were divorced. My father was very, very headstrong. My parent's marriage was not biblically based. And when I saw my father he taught me to run my household. You don't let anyone come in and tell you what to do. So when my husband and I got married I brought that luggage. I brought that mentality into the marriage and in the process I'm disrespecting him. And I understand what Eric says about roles. My role as a wife is to be supportive. If the husband is the head, then the wife is the neck which supports it. I should have his back. I shouldn't be stabbing him in the back and telling him what to do and disrespecting him; not allowing him to lead because that causes confusion. If you are taking that authority away from him and get in a situation where he needs to step up, he might step back and say no, you handle it. You can't have it both ways. You can't be the head of the household when it's convenient or when I feel it should be done. I've got to respect him in that role as the head of the household regardless of the situation. Now he will recognize my strengths and say "Honey, you're stronger in the area of finances so if I'm stronger with organizing or finances I need you to handle that but I'm not going to disrespect him in the process. I'm going to handle the bills, write them out. I'm going to take them to him and we're going to have that discussion; open that line of communication and make sure we're on one accord before we move forward.

Eric's view was the educational piece where it's like biblically based reprogramming.

In his words, "The woman has to know who she is; what a marriage is, and what a marriage is; defined biblically by God. And then, biblically, what are the husband and wife's role? There has to be some kind of foundation and that is the foundation defined by the bible. The past roles have to be completely erased. It's not what you learned in church growing up; it's not what you learned and what you saw in your parent's relationship because you know as an adult, it's distorted. And this is one reason why she became the dominant figure. I had to let her know that by being the head of the household, I have accountability. I'm solely responsible for my family. My wife is subject to me but again, we are subject to one another. And if God is in both of us; we should be equals in a sense - even though God put man responsible for his family.

As intelligent as I was in the natural I saw the term submission as a point of weakness. It wasn't until we were in church one Sunday morning and my Pastor began to break down how submission should be viewed from a place of strength instead of from a position of weaknesses. **It is very easy to use your tongue to tear down your spouse and correct them but it takes strength to be able to bridle your tongue especially when there are times in which you may not agree with a decision that your spouse has made.** It was that Sunday morning service that I began to change my perspective on submission and recognize that it was okay to submit to my husband and not do it from a place of weakness as if I were a doormat but to do it from a position of strength.

_____

_____

_____

_____

_____

How does a couple deal with each other's admitted flaws?

Recognize that we are all imperfect beings and discuss ways in which to compromise such that the outcome is favorable for both parties. Learn to pick and choose your battles wisely. Some disagreements aren't even worth the energy necessary to fight the battle.

Explain the difference between flaws vs. baggage?

One of my husband greatest flaws is that he loved to drop his clothes wherever they landed after work and collapse in the bed. It really got my temperature boiling. I yelled and screamed and got angry, he didn't want to have sex and guess what? It didn't change; it only caused a greater division between the two of us. It was during one of our monthly marriage ministry meeting that one of the facilitators began to talk about a concept in marriage. Do you want to be right or do you want to be happy? I began to realize that I was more upset about his laying on the bed and messing it up because I felt as if he didn't appreciate my hard work. I also began to reflect that was the way I gained my father's approval when I was younger. I kept my room clean and orderly. My husband messing it up just took me back to that point in my life that where I was seeking approval and little did I know that same thought pattern was being carried over into our marriage. His imperfections hit a trigger about my past that threatening to rob me of my future, so I had to retrain my way of thinking about certain behaviors.

Finding the bridge to each other again

Adultery is not just cheating on your spouse with another person. Rather, instead of cleaving to each other as man and wife, which God intended, there is a tendency to cleave to other things: children, jobs, ministries... These types of behaviors can cause your spouse to begin to question the marriage commitment. Feelings of neglect evolve into an emotional disconnect. Unfortunately, many couples do not have the tools or knowledge of how to effectively communicate with one another. Without references on how to address and overcome challenges in your relationship and without a solid foundation and no one to trust or talk to, resentment can develop and the gap widens, and with no bridge to each other, many couples separate and consider divorce. Divorce is not the only option. You can win in your marriage!!

On my second marriage with my first husband: by Guest Contributor

I've been married for 18 years and we've gone through a lot in our marriage. Our challenge came around that ten-year mark; there was a lot of unsettling behaviors in the marriage. We finally accomplished a lot of the things we said we would do together. My husband and I, we both got married fresh out of college. We were one of those couples who thought marriage was just for love and that with love, it would last. It wasn't a good idea. We got married after graduation; we got a job, had kids, and built a family. We got what we thought we're supposed to have. So I had built this marriage the way people told us the way marriage was supposed to be. We looked like our marriage as a success and people admired us. And I think it got to the point where I started realizing that there's something else that's supposed to be built, but it was missing. That something else is missing. And so it began to feel like we were building a lie. It really came down to commitment. There was separation in our marriage and that was even before the adultery took place. The adultery was part of the process. And the truth is, we just started to feel pinned down by our marriage or in his case; the ministry was his mistress. As he continued to move up in leadership, he would be away from home with the pastor helping him by leading a department or doing something for the auxiliary groups, and for what? It doesn't matter if he wasn't cheating on me but he was gone enough to make me feel like I was alone. It's just the fact that he had me thinking that I was number one and he barely had time for me. As a wife I'm looking at my child look at her daddy taking care of other children in the ministry and so I began to question it. I used to have the feeling and think to myself a lot of times, "This doesn't feel right." The bible says we should cleave to each other. But the truth is we cleaved to other things. It didn't matter what that other things were; it wasn't each other. We didn't realize the division it was causing and where it became the most visible. I remember one time; my husband was at the church. I called him and literally started yelling at him. He would walk other children home from church and literally walk them to our dinner table to eat. I very calmly told him you can have the church but this marriage? I don't want to be in it anymore. And it was really a turning point, I think, for him to begin to see what was going on. Because now that I've been here this whole time and I've been doing it all alone, you know for him, he's the man. He felt that he had it all figured out. **No, he didn't**. It took a while to realize we were connected to turmoil. And the turmoil got worse to the point where we ended up separated because everything changed for the worse. We arrived at the bridge that I think a lot of us crossed and began to erase our marriages' existence.

(It was a build-up) I reached my breaking point, I began to disconnect from my marriage emotionally, and I didn't that it could be restored. Even though he wanted to, know this, I neglected to let my feelings be known. We had a couple of people in our lives that would be there to support us but I felt that there are a lot of times where you need professional counseling because they're not biased and discuss things that we would feel comfortable about openly sharing. We ended up agreeing to a separation for about a year. And then I think a couple of months later his mother passed away and we lost my grandmother, who was like a mother to me. Soon after that, he lost his job and things weren't going so well at church. And so literally now, everything in our world was so tumultuous that by the time, I got to the point... I don't even know...It's indescribable. When I think about it, I don't even know how our situation affected our children because I was in the middle of a nervous breakdown. So I couldn't connect and started having trust issues with the people closest to me. But the truth is your husband is hurt because of what he's gone through. You're hurt because of what you've gone through. Two broken people trying to keep up a marriage does not fit well. I tried changing my perspective but it was hard.

Looking back, I can admit that I was insensitive to his commitment to ministry because I knew that he was raised in church all of his life. I felt that I was left emotionally vulnerable. I confided in someone and I fell for her all at the same time. So you say, well how did that happen? We worked together; she was a friend of mine. She was my confidant and the next thing I knew, we constantly spent a lot of time together. I nervously laugh about it today. We're like, how, and she was divorced about 12 years in to her marriage. She dated men and was attracted to them, so what made me so different; convenience. We would go out and have coffee, at the same time filling the void of loneliness for the both of us. It appeared that a woman who's finally listening and maintaining a friendship with me experienced what I went through. She actually became my "under cover" girlfriend. That is until I started to feel guilty and ashamed.

Knowing about people's past is so important to the success of a marriage because one of the things you realize is that people are searching for answers from their past and to heal their present circumstances. Everyone is walking around with questions and they're looking for answers but could never seem to find that peace within their hearts. And in my case, I was walking around with questions that when answered, would complete me. When vulnerable, this woman appeared to be the answer to my questions; she was wiser and she was relatable. She was about 12 years older than me so she had experienced more. Her input on my situation soothed my aching heart. I started allowing her to get closer to me. We went out to exclusive restaurants for dinner, she treated me well, and she had her corporate connections to look out for us. We would have VIP access to clubs and she took care of the expenses. I felt like a kid at Christmas time. She did everything my husband didn't do. I couldn't tell you the last time my husband took me out on a date. And now here I am being wooed by a woman. One day, we drove back to where my car was parked and she kissed me, I felt different. I felt good but I knew it wasn't right. I pulled back and was like whoa, now wait a minute! I'll never forget her response, "You're saying that now but your bodies saying something else. But it's okay. I'll wait until you're comfortable." My mind was saying NO but my body said YES! Whoa! It was one of those moments; I was confused. I remember telling my husband where we were broken so that we could fix it. Instead things got worse. That's how it was so easy for this woman to step in. So literally, we started an affair. **I share with people that it was not only the involvement, the physical interaction; it's about when we need that void filled and there's somebody else coming in to fill it.** Personally, it was the broken pieces in my childhood that had never been dealt with. And so my husband may not be responsible for what's going on because he was unaware of my past and the healing process that I needed to face before getting married.

When I was younger, my parents and my dad would go back and forth very often. I would go to the store and come back and my dad would be gone. I would go to a party the night before and I'd come back and he'd be gone. I would miss seeing him. The disappearing acts of my father caused me to spaz out because I felt that if my husband left, he would not return. At times I felt sick to my stomach. I felt mentally unstable; I didn't feel secure, or loved. My husband not being at home was unnerving to me. On the other hand, my husband is looking at the situation like you're angry so before I ever put my hands on you, I'll walk away because he witnessed abuse at an early age. As a result, **we were reacting to things from our childhood without a clue on how to react adults.** We both sought professional help because he wanted to work it out. I made up in my mind; I wanted a divorce. **He decided that he was going to fight for our marriage no matter how I felt.** He said that he wasn't leaving me and that he would do what it takes to change my mind. I still didn't budge. I had to learn that it was okay to walk away when things got a little heated and not feel lonely. We could have done a whole lot of walking away and making up if we knew that from the beginning, right?

In my opinion, **divorce is not an indication of two people not loving each other. It's more of them not knowing how to. I didn't know how to love him** the way that he needed to be loved and **I didn't know how to accept his love either. We didn't communicate with each other**; we instead fell in line with the routine of running our family and living our separate lives.

Ironically in my marriage I was the one that was pushing and advocating divorce. My husband interceded in prayer and convinced me to change my mind. One day he looked at me and said, **"I don't like who you are. I want the woman I married and I'm going to fight for that woman. I'm not walking away from my covenant. I am going to fight."** It was very difficult for me to accept and I think he noticed that. This caused him to open up in ways that I've never saw before. He showed me that his priority was our family. It was at the point that I decided to give him the chance that he deserved and not get a divorce. We went to counseling together. He started to take ownership and acknowledge where he needed to take the steps in being the best husband/father that he could be. I felt that had we not opened up our hearts to God and his teachings, seeing a professional would have never helped us in recovering our marriage. First of all, it's very hard to walk this road if you don't have two people who are trying to have a relationship with Christ. **Where he couldn't get through to me in prayer, the Holy Spirit could.** So if you've got two people that are trying to have a relationship with Christ it makes the process a whole lot easier. If you've got one person that may have that relationship and the other person that is kind of borderline; it's more difficult. Not all things are going to be reconciled because it takes two.

I thank God for my husband and his understanding of me and my past. I'm also thankful for the heart to forgive and become a better wife/mother. Today we are happily serving couples through ministry. I decided to share my story in hopes that it helps a couple in need of direction; in hopes of finding themselves and keeping their marriage whole.

Those were powerful words that shifted the trajectory to a path that lead back to each other. Their relationship was worth a second chance. Like a natural disaster destroying everything familiar, this was a chance to rebuild from the ground up with new tools, a solid foundation, and no outside influences from their past.

The first step was deciding to make a true effort to make their marriage work. With the help of a professional counselor, they realized their previous life was built on influences and examples from their youth; confided their problems with the wrong people, and tried to emulate someone else's perception of a happy, successful marriage.

Most people don't get divorced because they fall out of love. They get divorced because they don't know how to love one another to begin with. Remove all preconceived notions and open up the lines of real, soul-bearing communication. Hearing the truth might hurt but being lied to is destructive.

Surviving this process "Shawna" can joke and say she's married the second time with her first and only husband. To build that bridge to one another you must look the relationship directly in the eye and say, "I will fight for you. You are my covenant."

Your story may not be the same as Shawna's but we all have a story. It is our sincere desire for each and every person that reads this book to WIN in their marriage. We encourage you to continue to fight to overcome the challenges in marriage referred to as The Great Divide. We welcome the opportunity to celebrate your victories with you. Let's connect via Facebook, Twitter or you can follow us on Twitter or Periscope. We're rooting for you to win!!!

The ABC's of Marriage

*A*ffection is a very integral part of a marriage. It communicates love, support, protection and adoration of your spouse. Be mindful, that what we feed will grow. Healthy, frequent demonstrations of affection towards your spouse will help the marriage to grow. While one spouse may be more affectionate than the other, it is imperative find out the language of affection or love language that your spouse speaks in order for your method of delivery to be most impactful.

In what ways can you demonstrate a greater amount of affection towards your spouse?

_____

_____

_____

_____

_____

_____

_____

_____

_____

_____

_____

_____

***B**alance between work, family and marriage is critical. While the ability for a couple to provide for their family is very important, it is not a substitute for your presence in the home. A Marriage that is destined to win, needs to be recognized as even more valuable than the amount of money in a paycheck. We have all heard the cliché, "Work Hard play hard" but it is very crucial that the time that you invest in your spouse is not simply an afterthought. *Can you implement ways in which to balance your marriage and work, such as take shorter lunches? Minimize the amount of overtime worked?*

In what ways can you improve your Work/Life/Marriage Balance?

_____

_____

_____

_____

_____

_____

_____

_____

_____

Communication is Key.

Effective communication is a skill that all couples need to develop. It is not an overnight process. Open communication affords each spouse the opportunity to talk freely and openly, about their most private thoughts which includes but is not limited to their hopes, dreams, fears, challenges and/ or aspirations. Both discuss challenges and concerns in a respectful manner and refrain from utilizing hurtful or demeaning comments. Additionally, they are intentional about listening and comprehending their spouse's position even when their opinion differs.

In which way can you improve your ability to communicate with your spouse?

_____

_____

_____

_____

_____

_____

_____

_____

Dedication to your marriage **is essential**. I recently came across an image on the internet that had a picture of a couple walking together, carrying a raft over their heads and the caption read, *"Sink or Swim we're in this together".* This spoke volumes to me. I began to reflect on the state of many marriages today and how a greater degree of dedication is needed by both spouses in order to WIN. *How dedicated are you to your marriage? Do you have that same level of dedication that you once had when you first got married? What changes are you willing to make in order to get back to that?*

*E*ncourage one another **daily**. Nothing builds a spouse up more than a daily dose of encouragement from one's spouse. No one should be a greater cheerleader for your spouse than you are.

In what ways can you be an even better supporter or encourager for your spouse?

_____

_____

_____

_____

_____

_____

_____

*F*orgiveness is an essential key to any marriage.

"A happy marriage is the union of two good forgivers." -   Robert Quillen.

Remember, the purpose of walking in forgiveness is not for their sake, you forgive them for your sake. Forgiving doesn't mean forgetting, nor does it indicate that you condone what was said or done. It means that you have released the anger, guilt or frustration towards the offender.

_____

_____

_____

_____

_____

_____

_____

_____

_____

*G*rateful

How often do you express gratitude towards your spouse? Often times a couple will have settled down into a relationship and begin to take for granted the things that our spouses do on a daily basis. Don't forget to be grateful when your spouse does something around the house, or for you. It's the little things that when acknowledged by your spouse means the most.

_____

_____

_____

_____

_____

_____

_____

*H*onesty

Honesty is an integral part of your relationship. Your partner should be able to have confidence in not only what you say, but what you do. If this is an area in which you have had challenges previously I encourage you to be honest with your spouse.

_____

_____

_____

_____

_____

_____

_____

_____

_____

_____

*I*nitiate Intimacy with your **spouse.** It does not always have to be the husband. The wife and also help to establish a level of intimacy that makes her husband feel loved and desired both physically and emotionally. This type of connection can take your relationship to a whole different level.

What does intimacy look like in your eyes? Ask your spouse the same question. Where do the two of you agree? Disagree? What's your plan going forward to have more intimate moments as a husband and wife?

_____

_____

_____

*J*oy is a deeper feeling than "happiness;" whereas your degree of happiness can be impacted by financial status, health, or even day to day experiences. Those that have true joy in their marriage display an attitude that in spite of the current circumstances your attitude towards your spouse is not going to change.

Do you truly have Joy or do your emotions and attitudes fluctuate based on your circumstances? How can you change this?

_____

_____

_____

_____

_____

Kindness. In our marriages we

need to be intentional about demonstrating kindness towards our spouses. This is a great way to fill up the love tank of our spouse. *What acts of kindness can you show to your spouse today and on a daily basis going forward?*

_____

_____

_____

_____

_____

_____

_____

_____

_____

Love each other beyond our **faults.** Each and every one of us, no matter how wonderful we feel that we are, we are still imperfect beings. We are going to miss the mark and say or do something that may annoy or irritate or spouse. The key is how do you love them through their faults? When their imperfections begin to surface, what is your response? Is this the same way that you would want to be treated?

How have you loved your spouse beyond their faults?

_____

_____

_____

_____

Manage your finances **wisely.** Money or the lack thereof, is one of the top three reasons that there is what we refer to as "The Great Divide" in Marriage. So before you create any additional expenses in your marriage, have a conversation with your spouse regarding the impact this expense can have on the two of you.

Are the two of you on the same page in regards to your finances?

If so, write a note below about your successes in the area of finances. If not, make some notes on how the two of you can overcome this challenge as a couple. Don't forget to refer to our section on finances if you need any suggestions.

_____

_____

_____

_____

_____

_____

_____

_____

Never stop dating your spouse! Did you know that going out on dates regularly with your spouse, not only helps to reduce stress, but it also gives you the chance to focus on one another on a regular basis? This opens the door for enhanced communication and greater levels of intimacy.

When was the last time you dated your spouse? What did you do?

_____

_____

_____

*O*neness is not optional, it's mandatory. **Genesis 2:24** says that the man and wife became "one flesh.". There should be unity within the marriage, operating on one accord. "**One flesh**" means so much more than just the physical union between husband and wife sexually; it's an emotional connection and spiritual connection as well.

Are you and your spouse operating in oneness?

_____

_____

_____

_____

_____

_____

Prioritize your marriage **first.** I can't stress this enough. A baby sitter is much less expensive than a divorce attorney. In order to maintain the oneness that we just talked about, it is essential that the two of you nurture your marriage. After God, the next in line is your marriage. Nope - not the kids or that job, or even your church duties. Yes, we said it!!! Whatever you feed will grow.

Are you feeding your marriage or is it in starvation mode?

_____

_____

_____

_____

_____

Quality time is essential.

Finding moments for quality time to connect with your spouse will take some time to plan, so we must be intentional in this endeavor. This does not happen on its own. Quality time presents opportunities for a couple to grow both together and individually. These opportunities help to fortify the marriages for the long haul. Remember marriage is a marathon not a sprint. It takes time and preparation in order to succeed.

What do you consider to be "quality time with your spouse"? How often do you and your spouse have quality time together?

_____

_____

_____

_____

_____

_____

_____

_____

_____

_____

Respect for one another is **mandatory.** There are numerous ways in which we demonstrate respect for our spouse. Here are just a few 1) Choose your words wisely (Words DO HURT!) 2) Acknowledge the contributions to the household 3) Be willing to compromise (We all have feelings) 4) Be considerate and 5) Be willing to admit when you have made a mistake. These are just a few of the many ways in which you can show respect for your spouse.

What are some of the ways on which you show respect for your spouse that are not listed above?

_____

_____

_____

_____

_____

_____

_____

_____

_____

_____

_____

Submit. I know that this may been seen in some households as a curse word. :) LOL. Believe it or not it was in our household as well. It wasn't until it was explained to me that submission comes from a place of strength. It is strength that is harnessed. It is very easy to kick someone when they are down. It is a far greater challenge to be silent or walk away; even when you feel entitled to do so. While it can be challenging to tame the tongue, it can be done.

Has submission ever been a challenge in your household? How did the two of you handle it?

---

*T*rust. Once trust has been it can take quite some time to be re-established. The good thing is that it is an obstacle that can be overcome, in time. Think of an example of how you have to help rebuild the trust in your marriage or relationship and what steps you implemented in order to do so.

_____

_____

_____

_____

_____

Understanding is extremely important when it comes to a having a healthy, successful marriage that can win. A husband and wife that are willing to be understanding each others' differences and idiosyncrasies will have a greater level of commitment to their marriage, even in the midst of life's challenges.

In what ways have you had to be understanding of your spouse? How has that helped you to grow as a couple?

Vision for your Marriage.

What is the vision for your marriage? Where do the two of you see yourselves one year from now? Five years from now? Ten years from now? In order to avoid division in the home the two of you need to have the same vision for your marriage.

When was the last time the two of you discussed the vision for your marriage? Has anything changed? As we grow and mature, or as life experiences occur, we may have to go back to the blue print for our marriage and make sure that the two of you are on track. If not, what happened? What steps are you prepared to take to get back on track?

Wisdom. Use wisdom in your thoughts and actions. Treat your spouse with the same level of respect and love that you would want them to treat you with.

In what areas of your marriage could you use more wisdom?

_____

_____

_____

_____

_____

_____

_____

_____

_____

E**X**_press what you expect._ Often times in marriage on spouse harbors ill feelings or resentment towards the other spouse because of unmet needs however, what they didn't consider is that, the information was never communicated to their spouse. In any relationship it is extremely important that you maintain an open dialogue with your spouse. Take the time necessary to clearly communicate you needs to your spouse. Remember your spouse cannot meet a need that has not been expressed.

_____

_____

_____

_____

_____

Y_es_ **is a powerful Word!** I want you to commit to being more positive in your marriage for the next 7 days. Try saying Yes to spending more time with your spouse. Commit to saying yes to watching a football game with your husband or shopping with you wife. The commitment to being more positive in your relationship and saying yes instead of no for change can bring about a tremendous difference. I understand that it may be a little uncomfortable at first; however, you are planting a seed.   Saying **"Yes"** instead of "**No**" is an investment in the future of your relationship.

What three things can you commit to saying yes to that you have previously said no to?

_____

_____

_____

_____

_____

_____

_____

Zeal for one another. Challenges may come and go, jobs houses, cars, etc. All of those things may come and go. Remember they are just things!!! Things that can be replaced!!!!Never lose your zeal for one another. You have worked hard to build a lasting relationship; now don't let that fire go out.

Think about 2-3 ways in which you have lost your zeal for your spouse and your relationship. Commit today to making changes and being intentional about the zeal that you have for your marriage.

_____

_____

_____

_____

Special Thank You

To Members of the Five Fold Ministry that have poured
into us over the years: Pastor Riva Tims, Pastor Idella
McIntyre, Pastor Patrick & Lady Angela Ligon, Pastor
Wanda Tommie, Pastor Kim Gragston, Mother Christine
McGlothine-Moore, Dr. Genevia Boyd, and Apostle Anthony
Earl, your prayers, words of encouragement and passion
for the things of God have had a tremendous impact on
our lives. We thank you all for encouraging us to walk into
our calling and utilizing the gifts that God has placed on
the inside of us.

Made in the USA
Middletown, DE
13 August 2022